CORNELL AND ITHACA
in Postcards

ITHACA BELLES

A favorite marketing scheme of postcard publishers has always been the "stock card" design, to which the name of any community could be printed. It is clear that any convenient scene could be placed in the box where the Cornell Arts quadrangle appears, and the name changed from "Ithaca" to whatever town offered a chance to make sales. After all, every "burg" from Auburn to Zelionople has its pretty girls!

BEAUTIFUL GORGES

In recent years area automobiles have sported bumper stickers with the message "ITHACA IS GORGES". It may be a bad pun, but it's the truth! Anyone who has ever had the privilege of living in the community can always relate to the scenic beauties of the region as exemplified by the many deep cuts that waterways have made as they wend their way from the hillsides through the rocky terrain eventually to empty into Cayuga Lake. The power house below Sibley Falls was built in 1904 to house two Pelton water wheels each turning a 150 kilowatt generator, and for many years it supplied all of Cornell's electricity needs. (more on page 87, upper picture)

CORNELL AND ITHACA
in Postcards

ENTRANCE TO THE CAMPUS IN WINTER. CORNELL UNIVERSITY.

HARVEY N. ROEHL

TAYLOR TRADE PUBLISHING
LANHAM • NEW YORK • BOULDER • TORONTO • PLYMOUTH, UK

Copyright © 1986, 2009 by the Estate of Harvey N. Roehl
First Taylor Trade Publishing edition 2009

Published by Taylor Trade Publishing
An imprint of The Rowman & Littlefield Publishing Group, Inc.
4501 Forbes Boulevard, Suite 200, Lanham, Maryland 20706
www.rlpgtrade.com

Estover Road, Plymouth PL6 7PY, United Kingdom

Distributed by NATIONAL BOOK NETWORK

Library of Congress Cataloging-in-Publication Data

Roehl, Harvey N.
  Cornell and Ithaca in postcards / Harvey N. Roehl.
     p. cm.
  Originally published: Vestal, N.Y. : Vestal Press, 1986.
  Includes bibliographical references.
  ISBN 978-1-58979-425-2 (pbk. : alk. paper)
  1. Ithaca (N.Y.)—Pictorial works. 2. Cornell University—Pictorial works. 3. Postcards—New York (State)—Ithaca. I. Title.
  F129.I8R64 2009
  974.7'710410222—dc22
                                        2009006357

Manufactured in the United States of America.

FOREWORD

History comes in many forms. In this book our local history is presented by means of picture postcards. This is not a broadly speculative view of the past, nor is it one that is thematic. Rather, this is history in its most particular form.

Postcard views of a community usually depict notable buildings and natural wonders; as you will see, our postcard history also commemorates buildings, events and sights that might also be called mundane. Yet, postcards were commercial items and it did no one any good if they were unappealing to the public. The cards seen here were created, bought, and sent or collected. At the time when they were printed they were seen as representative of the area: today they are collectors items.

Government issued postcards had their origin in Austria in 1869 when the *Korrespondenz Karte* was issued. Some years earlier in the United States, John P. Charlton of Philadelphia obtained a copyright for a privately printed card decorated with a small pattern. In 1873 the United States government issued postal cards of its own costing one penny each. These were stamped on one side where the address would be added, and plain on the reverse side.

Picture postcards in the United States date from 1893. At first these cards carried a picture on one side, the stamp and address on the reverse and the only space on which to write was on the border. These cards cost two cents to send —twice the amount of the government card—until 1898 when all post cards could be mailed for one penny. In 1907 the United States Postal Service allowed writing on a postcard next to the address, a regulation popular with all the manufacturers of picture postcards and those people with a message to send.

The postcards that tell our local history are views of natural wonders found in the area and of buildings, trains, bridges, street scenes, and other evidences of a progressive society. Many of the early picture postcards were printed in Germany and England, resulting in some peculiar spellings (lower, p.28) and in some curious scenes. Postcard artists often added features to a local scene or deleted something in the belief that they were creating a better image. This tampering with the actual is not new. When William H. Walton made his lithographs of Ithaca in the 1830's and 1840's, he added rather large ships to one view to indicate a commerce on Lake Cayuga that had not yet occurred and never was to be. (see lower cards, p. 35 and 43)

There are also a few gag cards included here: cards fit to be used anywhere with space for a town's name, or cards that show such a universal sight that they might be used in any hometown.

These cards also depict change. Some commemorate a scene that is now gone from our experience of life here, others show the transformation of a local institution. So we can see a picture of the Ithaca hospital on Aurora Street, and later the new hospital on Quarry Street; the first building is gone, the Quarry Street hospital is now the home of Ithacare.

It is interesting to speculate on the subjects selected for picture postcards. Many are scenes we would never ourselves find attractive: a house in ruins, an ordinary building, churches, a dormitory. If you look on postcard racks in Ithaca today, some cards illustrate our most important local buildings while the greatest number depict the scenic wonder of our area. But look closely, and you will also find a number of contemporary gag cards — so some things never change!

So enjoy this view of Cornell University and Ithaca around the turn-of-the-century—the old cars, the new street lights, the trolleys, the trains—the landmarks of an era now gone, an era that can still be recalled fondly by many and a time commemorated on picture postcards for everyone.

Carol Kammen
Ithaca, New York

THANKS TO THOSE WHO HELPED

This book makes no claim to original research; most facts have been gleaned from books by various authors, as noted in the bibliography. The concept, organization, and an occasional thinly-disguised opinion are the writer's.

Special acknowledgement must be made to the late Morris Bishop, whose book *A History of Cornell* is an absolute delight to read, and to Professor Kermit Carlyle Parsons of Cornell's Department of Architecture whose detailed study *The Cornell Campus—A History of Its Planning and Development* provided a great many facts used here . . . and of course to The Cornell University Press, publishers of both, for permission to make direct quotations.

Also thanks are due to Harold Cox, publisher of Richard Kerr's *The Ithaca Street Railway* for permission to quote from that book, and to Darwin Publishers for permission to quote from Robert Archer's *The Lehigh Valley*.

Ithaca and Its Past, by Daniel Snodderly, published by the DeWitt Historial Society, was of great help in regard to downtown buildings, and I express thanks both to the author and the organization for the use this material.

Special thanks must go to Carol Kammen, author, historian and teacher who is well-known to Ithacans for her interesting articles on local history that appear frequently in *The Ithaca Journal*. Mrs. Kammen gave generously of her time to review the entire manuscript and she offered many helpful editorial and historical suggestions.

Many other people helped in various ways—loaning individual cards, checking on specific questions, providing information, and so forth: Jack Garside, Herbert Trice, Alan Dixon, the staff of the Broome County Public Library, Herbert B. Hartwig Jr., Jack Perry, Samuel Cloyes, Jonathan Rook, Henry L. Clark, John Bennison, Rev. Bernard Carges, Q. David Bowers, Louis Goodwin, Joan K. FitzGerald, Ed Hartz, Donald Stinson, William Reed Gordon, Harold Andrews, Robert Fiske, Bruce Tracy, Jim Sherman, and last but not least, Gil Williams for his help in proofreading and his many constructive suggestions regarding content and form. I've tried hard not to leave anyone out, but if I have, please let me know so proper acknowledgement can be made in a subsequent printing.

Several of the cards used in the book are from the author's collection, but over half are from the private collection of Tom and Sally McEnteer of Catatonk, New York, who were not only generous in making available their rare and valuable cards, but they put at my disposal their magnificent library on Ithaca, Cornell, and Tompkins County. A second large group of cards was made available by Adam Perl, whose antique shop Pastimes Antiques in Ithaca's DeWitt Mall is a delight to visit. Mr. Perl is one of the finest dealers in postcards in the northeast. Special thanks are owed to these folks, whose interest in preserving and disseminating knowledge of our regional history is truly outstanding.

Harvey N. Roehl
Vestal, New York
Summer 1986

Adam Perl, owner of Pastimes Antiques, The DeWitt Mall, Ithaca

Sally and Tom McEnteer, Catatonk, New York

Designed and composed by Eastern Graphics of Binghamton, New York in 9 point Palatino, 1 point leaded, with display lines in Palatino Bold and Rustikalis Modernized Gothic.

Harvey Roehl as a youngster

GROWING UP IN ITHACA . . .
in the 1920's, '30's, and '40's.

My father and mother, together with their 5-year old son John, moved to Ithaca from Wauwautosa, Wisconsin, in 1917. Dad had been invited to come to Cornell's burgeoning College of Agriculture to set up a course in what was then known as "farm mechanics", so he rented a house on Bryant Avenue and went to work. He told me that after he had been in Ithaca a couple of years the dean of the college called him in and said "Roehl, we like your work. I suggest you build a house and plan to stay" (or words to that effect). So, having once written a book on house construction, it was a simple matter for him to supervise the work of a group of subcontractors in building a fine new home of his design on Oxford Place; he did all the interior finishing work, with the finest in oak floors and trim. The house was completed in 1923; I made my appearance the following year.

Dad was on the Cornell faculty for 33 years, until his retirement in 1948. He and Mom were midwesterners; first-generation Americans of German immigrant parents who had settled in Wisconsin and Minnesota, and they said they'd never move east. But they always knew they had made the right move when they settled in Ithaca. They loved the place!

Being raised in a university community doesn't make a person better than anyone else, but it surely does have its advantages. People are education-oriented, which means the young are exposed to learning about many things. My playmates were more often than not the children of faculty parents, and one way or another, a little knowledge about many different fields brushed off on all of us. Allen Blodgett's dad was an expert on potatoes; Larry Burrows' father was an authority on bridges. Harold Fitzpatrick's father was a mushroom scientist, and George and Gifford Briggs' dad was a renowned physical chemist. Chuck Spaeth's father was a professor of forestry. Gene Crosby's father was an entomologist, a spider man. And so it went.

And almost all the kids I grew up with developed hobbies of one sort or another that led to their careers. Like Paul Kelsey, who was always studying birds. He became a well-known wildlife biologist and naturalist. Tony Ceracche, who with George Briggs built a tiny television set back in the 1930's . . . Tony made his fortune in Ithaca's cable TV; George became a scientist with RCA labs. Bob Trousdale, who was always fiddling with electrical stuff. . . went on to become a highly successful electrical engineer. Doug Dallenbach, who was always looking through microscopes, became a renowned pathologist. And Harold Andrews, who was always studying the technology of aircraft, became a successful aeronautical engineer and also a recognized authority on U.S. naval aviation history. . . the pattern repeated itself over and over, to the point where today I enjoy knowing about those all-too-few youngsters of today who go after a hobby with a passion. There's no doubt in my mind that a college environment helps develop this trait.

Most parents before World War II were determined to have their kids exposed to music. Mine trotted me off to Mrs. Hattie Stewart, the neighborhood piano teacher when I was five, for what was the start of a life-long involvement with that instrument. The Ithaca School system offered a superb music program to its students, and many of my friends became proficient on various band and orchestral instruments. Many of us were exposed to the great concert artists who visited and performed at Cornell. Marian Anderson, Joseph Hofmann, Albert Spaulding, Yehudi Menuhin, José Iturbi and Paul Robeson are but a few we enjoyed and remembered.

Frances Parker, who lived next door, was my brother's age; they both were really good at playing popular tunes of the 1920's on the piano. I held out the hope that one day I would be able to play that same stuff as well, so I practiced hard for years. My Dad hated jazz, and I'm sure my efforts grated on his nerves, but the practice paid off for me and being able to play this music has provided years of personal pleasure. I recommend it, if you can get your own kids to practice!

Probably my first recollection of Ithaca as such was a view from the window of a Pullman car in the early morning, coming down the DL & W switchback on South Hill. I was returning at age 4 with my parents from a trip to England where Dad worked for a year, setting up a course of instruction at the Dartington School in Devon. The school was an experimental one, established by Mr. and Mrs. Leonard Elmhirst, she being the former Mrs. Willard Straight. This trip may or may not have been what influenced my enjoyment of railroading, but readers of this book will surely detect such a pursuasion in the pages ahead.

Another fleeting recollection, from that same year of 1928, was seeing the State Theatre under construction, and noticing welders working on the trolley car tracks in the middle of State Street. Maybe these glimpses helped to nurture my life-long enthusiasms for movie palaces and trolley cars.

Belle Sherman School was very new when I attended grades K through 6. As is so often the case, the things one recalls tend to be trivial, like when Miss Richards, the principal, would see kids fighting in the schoolyard. She'd open her office window and ring a big handbell; that was the signal that enough was enough. And of course Mrs. White, our fifth-grade teacher, whose son became a prominent local nurseryman. She frequently would say to us "Now young people, you cannot learn to roller-skate by sitting on the front porch and watching the other children go up and down the sidewalk." What a marvelously sensible piece of advice, advice I've always tried to put to use these many years since.

And who could forget the days at Frank David Boynton Junior High School? Miss Bartholomew, the principal, was a little bit of a woman who ran a very tight ship. My first day there included attending an assembly program, with a chap named Edward Eddy making a campaign speech for a 9th-grade class office. I don't remember what he said, but he left a positive impression. And he went on to become the President of the University of Rhode Island, so apparently he kept on impressing people.

And then there was Miss Sweitzer, who taught vocal music and conducted the chorus. When we as a class would misbehave, she would lose her temper, get red in the face, and shriek at us. Naturally we considered this great fun, and an inducement to provoke additional confrontations. And Mr. McIntyre, who after a year of Social Studies said to us: "I'll be happy if you have learned one thing from this year. And that is don't believe everything you read, just because it's in print." More sound advice! And Mr. Judway, who always looked like a fashion plate, with every hair in place, moustache neatly trimmed, etc. Years later we met when we were buck privates in the Army; we both looked a little scroungy and disheveled. Then we were equals in life.

Only as we grow older, do we begin to appreciate the efforts of the adults who tried to mold good citizens out of such raw material. Folks like Mr. and Mrs. Ed Hile, Joshua Cope and Professor Perry who worked so hard as scout leaders in my youth, and people like Mrs. Grant Potter who always conducted our elementary Sunday school class and who did her best to teach us the difference between right and wrong. Everyone's home town has good people like these, most of whom are seldom recognized for their countless contributions.

For many of us neighborhood kids close to the campus, the chance to drive our coaster wagons around the sidewalks of Cornell—especially the "Ag" campus—at a time when automobile traffic was still light made for countless enjoyable hours. And later, carrying two newspaper routes on campus greatly increased my familiarity with the place long before my student days.

My parents loved to picnic, and in those days before air conditioning was available to the masses, we frequently would drive out to Taughannock or Enfield Park to take a swim in Cayuga Lake or in the pool just below Enfield Falls. Then a pleasant evening meal, with hamburgers or hot dogs cooked over an open fire amidst refreshing breezes from Cayuga or under the trees at Enfield. It was always cool and comfortable on the hottest of days. I think serving in the Army in the 1940's cured a lot of us from the kick out of eating "in the open" in later years.

Dad loved to travel, and always considered it an "investment"—not in dollars, but in the joys of recollection to be had in subsequent years. By the time I was of high school age, I'd travelled in 40 states and had seen much of their individual brand of scenery—very little of which outstripped what we had right around Ithaca. Different, of course, but not necessarily any more satisfying.

The family wasn't much on boating, but occasionally some friends of my parents would invite us for an outing on the lake in their cruiser or speedboat, and that was thrilling for a youngster. And we had plenty of friends who would have us out at their lakefront cottages for an evening, and this generally meant a chance to go row-boating — not as exciting as speedboating, but still loads of fun.

What a wonderful bunch of kids went to Ithaca High in the time of the class of '41! Who will ever forget the infectious smiles of Jimmy Miller and Ronnie Garside? So many insignificant things stick in my mind. . . like the time that Pat Landon (I think it was, whose father was a professor of drama at Ithaca College), who organized a funny assembly skit one day, called the *Raisins of Anger*. Seems he had just read the current best-selling novel, *The Grapes of Wrath*. Chet Sarsfield and I could both wiggle our Adam's apples; when German teacher Oswald Laubenstein would get angry at our class for misbehaving, we'd both bob our neckties up and down (yes, we wore ties in those days). Mr. Laubenstein would always lose his stern composure on seeing us and would break up in laughter, and then we'd all go back to work. And Leonard Buyse, who also taught German, was pretty handy on the basketball floor. We called him 'The Flying Deutschman.'

I well recall Mr. Butler's valiant efforts to teach "Horner's method for irrational roots" to dunderheads like Jack Slade and me in his intermediate algebra class. Jack and I used to study together in the evening but in reality what we shared was our mutual ignorance. And there was Miss Wager, who we always figured was as old as the ancient history she taught. She must have weighed 90 pounds, and we were all scared to death of her. And Miss Claflin, who many thought was the best math teacher ever invented.

And Fred Stutz, who went on to become Dean of Cornell's Department of Education, who taught American history. One day he spent an entire hour talking about the new "Townsend Plan" idea, whereby everyone over 60 would get from the government a pension of $200 per month that they had to spend, putting money back into the economy. This was to lead to unparalled prosperity; the factories would be busy, the farmers would be making money again, everyone would be back on "easy street", so to speak. He built it up and made it sound wonderful. Just before the class ended he said "There's only one thing they haven't figured out yet . . . and that's where to get the money." Now *there* was a splendid teacher.

Dayton F. Latham was the band director and teacher at Ithaca High. A strange man, some of us thought, but later we band members realized that he had indeed given us a fine appreciation of musicianship. With Ithaca College's excellent Department of Music right across the street, we were all exposed in a variety of ways to quality.

One time a small circus came to perform in the auditorium. For publicity, they had a air-operated calliope on the back of a truck, and Art Buckingham got to play it all up and down the streets of town. Boy, was I envious. At age 60 I finally bought one that once belonged to the Ringling Circus, so now I can play it all the time. Eat your heart out, Art Buckingham!

Henry Clark and I were always building motorscooters. Many a day we'd arrive at school all grimy with grease and dirt from trying to make them function properly on the early morning trip. It got so we were congratulated on the days when we arrived unblemished. And he and I would more often ride our scooters (or bicycles) to the Lehigh Station during lunch hours, to watch the noon train come down the hill from Buffalo and Trumansburg. We were startled the day the train was headed by a newly-streamlined steam locomotive, painted in Cornell's colors! Later, when we had access to cars, we'd often go down by the Inlet late at night to watch Number 4 drag down the hill, its steel wheels for the full length of the train "rimmed with fire" from the friction of the brakes. What a spectacular sight. For a time, Hank had a '29 Cord convertible sedan that had cost him a couple of hundred bucks. Eventually he sold it for $40, and the best chance he ever had to get rich was gone. Today it's easily a $100,000 car.

Kids enjoy having their own "hang-out". Oliver (Bud) Jones, Paul Sharp, Fred Spry, Al Rasmussen, Henry Clark, and I and numerous others "hung out" at Bill Cooper's gas station, at the corner of Ithaca Road and Maple Avenue. He put us to work, too; we learned how to grease cars and wait on customers. But best of all we were exposed to his unique brand of humor. If you didn't have a sense of humor, you soon developed one from "Coopie." My brother's "hang-out" was Petrillose's barber shop on College Avenue. Not half as much fun as being able to fool around with customer's cars, I always thought.

I became a Cornell student in 1941, when Freshmen still wore "beanies" and World War II was already raging in Europe. It was an uneasy time when our futures were uncertain, and already some friends were signing up with the services as well as the Canadian Air Force. Engineering school was a real grind for me with my limited capabilities in mathematics, and I don't have a lot of memories of frivolity during that period in my life. In December of '41 the United States entered the war, and the campus was a pretty serious place with the Navy bringing in hordes of Ensigns for training under the V-12 program, temporary buildings being erected to house big diesel engines used by the Navy, and everyone wondering what was in store for us as individuals.

One diversion was playing in the ROTC band; as a sophomore I was in the "Big Red Band" that marched and played at football games in what was then considered a most unusual "ten-square" formation, with an even 100 musicians. Learning and executing the pictorial routines for the half-time shows was surely interesting, as were the trips, of which we were able to make only two. By 1942 the war effort had severely restricted travel, so the Dartmouth game was held in Buffalo, of all places. Apparently the reasoning was that at least there it was possible to produce a crowd to fill the UB stadium, whereas few people would have been able to drive to New Hampshire. It was so cold the ground was frozen, and the team had to wear sneakers in place of spiked shoes, and playing my metal clarinet was clearly impossible. All I could do was to fake it. (we won, 21-19). And of course we made the traditional trip to Philadelphia, via train, to play Pennsylvania on Thanksgiving Day.

Of course no student of engineering from that era will ever forget Professor Grantham's superb demonstration lectures in physics, nor will I ever fail to recall the fascinating lectures by Professor John R. Bangs on Industrial Organization and Management. Nor will I fail to remember my concern as to whether I would ever make it all the way to become a graduate engineer.

The war did intervene, of course, and I was trained as a technician in that new, then-highly secret "radar", as used on the B-29's that waged destruction on the Japanese homeland. This isn't the place to get into war stories, but I know that it never occurred to me at any time that America would be anything but victorious in this horrendous struggle.

A lot of fine young men from our high school class paid the price of liberty in World War II. Bob Heidt, lost in tank warfare in Germany; Steve Weatherby, downed while flying a B-26 against Hitler's hordes; talented artist John Krist, who drew the cartoons in our year book, killed while a gunner on a Navy plane; Jack Hart, lost in Germany. Not the whole list, but four too many. Ithaca didn't forget us when we went off to war. The Chamber of Commerce organized volunteers to put together a bi-weekly newsletter that was sent to Ithacans all over the world, to whomever they had an address. Those of us in the service sent cards with new addresses and maybe a tid-bit of information to the Chamber as we were shifted about the globe, and this information was always printed in the newsletter, thus enabling Ithacans to keep in touch. In the far Pacific on Guam, Bud Jones, Bob Zahn, Fred Spry, Bud Cornelius, Hugh Troy (the famed practical joker), your writer, and numerous others used to get together regularly and collectively wish we were all back home. I recall that many of my buddies in the Air Force were puzzled by this; many didn't understand why we would get together merely on the basis of having come from a common place. They would have, had they been from Ithaca.

Perhaps my favorite course after returning to Cornell was a graduate course in Automotive Engineering, taught by Professor Louis Otto, to a small group of us who had enthusiasm for the subject. He knew a lot of "biggies" in the field, so amidst our studies of the mathematics of automotive design, we took some invaluable field trips: like going to Buffalo to see the production facilities of the "Playboy" car (nothing to do with Hugh Hefner); to Syracuse to the engine factory owned by the Tucker organization (another ill-fated post-World War II attempt at building a car); and to Elmira to learn all about how American-LaFrance fire engines were constructed. In each case we met with the executives involved, and learned all the "inside dope" on the various products.

Cornell was quite a different place after the World War II, and has been so ever since. When I was growing up in its environs, it was quiet, sort of "laid-back", with what seemed to a youngster to have a lot of "fun" things taking place all the time. Fraternity rushing, Spring Days, crew races, ball games (while never a sports buff, I do recall seeing Walter Johnson play a demonstration game at Hoy Field with the Cleveland Indians, a fact that recently made me a sort of hero with the kids next door who are real baseball fans) and just lots of goings-on that were easy to take. Cornell today is almost a separate city, with parking problems, student demonstrations taking place from time to time, the greenery being gobbled up by new construction, and all the headaches that go with a population of four or five times what is was 50 years earlier.

Perhaps this is why I have derived so much pleasure in assembling this book; it has afforded an amateur historian an excuse to take a look at the days of his youth and a bit earlier. Looking through and selecting postcard views from the hundreds made available to me has been sheer joy; digging out the facts and writing about them to accompany the scenes has only added to the pleasure.

There's really no end to one's reminiscing and sadly only a few people have been mentioned, when by all rights there should be scores, if not hundreds, cited among those who have been positive influences. It has been said that one's personality is the sum total of the personalities a person has been exposed to in his lifetime. If this is the case, I'm lucky to have had so many friends in Ithaca. I can't think of a place I would rather have been brought up or gone to school in than Ithaca and Tompkins County!

Harvey Roehl as an oldster

The author:

Harvey N. Roehl was born and raised in Ithaca, attended the Ithaca Public Schools, and graduated from Ithaca High in 1941. He entered Cornell that year, and graduated from the Sibley School of Mechanical Engineering 8 years later, with an interruption for military service. After brief stints in industry, he held a variety of teaching and administrative positions at Broome Community College in Binghamton, New York over a 21-year period. He has a Master's Degree in Education from Cornell, is a Licensed Professional Engineer in New York State and a Major in the U.S. Air Force Reserve (retired). Besides being a private pilot, he has done all sorts of interesting things, including the building of an extensive collection of antique automatic musical instruments. In 1961 he and his wife Marion started The Vestal Press Ltd., on a part-time basis, and since 1973 have made it their sole occupation. The firm specializes in books and publications on antiquarian technical hobbies such as player pianos, music boxes, carousels, theatre pipe organs, Victorian parlor organs, and antique radios.

August 22-29, 1906

Home, home, sweet sweet home;

Ithaca, N.Y., East Hill from South Hill

Six-mile Creek, the source of Ithaca's water supply, runs in the gorge in the foreground of this picture. The Columbia street bridge crosses it. Cornell's Library and McGraw Hall towers are prominent on the skyline, as is a large unidentified structure close to the right of the photo. The "new" city hospital was built just across the gorge, to the right in the picture, on Quarry Street. Years ago the Ithaca city fathers on special wintry occasions temporarily closed Columbia Street so that Ithaca small fry could coast down that steep slope. Your writer has fond memories of zipping a good distance across the bridge before the slope-imparted momentum of his Flexible Flyer with its one passenger became exhausted, bringing the sled to a halt. What fun trudging back up the hill to see if maybe next time a few feet farther might be in the offing! The musical staff of "Home, Sweet Home" was the logo adopted by the committee promoting "Old Home Week", a local festivity marked by difficulty in raising funds to carry it out, and the sudden failure of the pipe organ in the Presbyterian Church when a large throng had assembled to hear a recital by Professor George M. Chadwick of Boulder, Colorado. Contemporary accounts in the *Ithaca Daily Journal* would suggest that aside from these minor setbacks, a good time was had by all who attended.

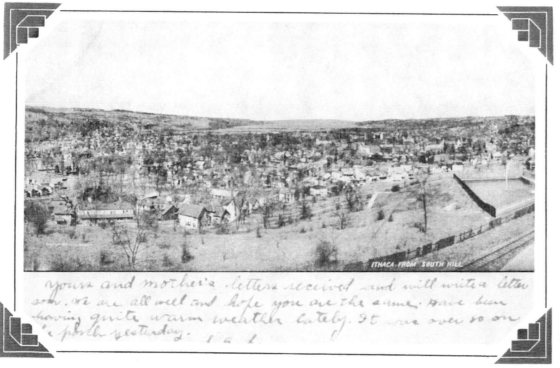

ITHACA FROM SOUTH HILL

Picture post cards were first introduced in America in 1893 during the Columbian Exposition, but it wasn't until 1907 that Congress gave authority to the Post Office to permit messages to be written on the address side of the card. Between these dates messages had to be squeezed onto whatever slim margin that publishers made available on the side or bottom of the card, and this one featuring a dandy view looking north from South Hill is an excellent example. Note the Lackawanna Railroad tracks at the lower right at a location just west of today's Borg-Warner plant. The trains to Owego originally surmounted the hill with a series of inclined planes which hoisted individual cars. This picture is of the later configuration whereby the tracks made a switch-back to gain the altitude. The rails we see here are on the lower part of this traverse. From this point the tracks made a sweeping curve to the left, and back into the picture again at far-left center.

City Hall, Ithaca, N. Y.

Erected in 1844 at the corner of Seneca and Tioga Streets to serve as town hall and firehouse, this sturdy Greek Revival building of stone and wood stood for 122 years until demolished as obsolete in 1966, giving way to the Seneca Street parking ramp . . . an action which brought about the founding of Historic Ithaca, Inc., whose mission is to preserve historic landmarks. [Write-up from The Tompkins County Trust Company Landmark Series, 1978]. In 1896 the Women's Christian Temperance Union erected the public drinking fountain as a means of encouraging the consumption of water, rather than alcohol. The statue is of Hebe, the goddess of youth and cup bearer of the immortals "who had the power of making the aged young again.".

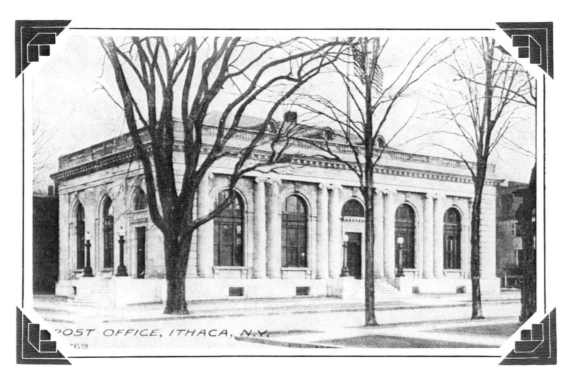

POST OFFICE, ITHACA, N.Y.

In 1908 the post office moved from its Colonial Building location on State Street to this fine new Beaux Arts style structure. James Knox Taylor, the federal architect, is credited by Dan Snodderly with this masterful design involving "large Ionic columns, elaborate arched windows, a fan-shaped decorative grill over the main entrance, a handsome frieze, a roof balustrade, and dormers. Inside are vaulted ceilings and marble wall facings." It was built to serve a long time.

The Hospital Association, formed in 1889, was presented with the Burt mansion in 1890 for use as a hospital. Located on North Aurora Street at Cascadilla Creek, it was not long in service before additions were necessary — specifically a ward for contagious diseases and a home for nurses, followed by an operating room annex. By 1910 it was obvious that the facility was outmoded, and efforts were started to construct a new building.

In 1910, a citizen's committee of 150, headed by Jacob Rothschild, raised $130,000 to construct "The New City Hospital" on Quarry Street, with Gibb and Waltz as the architects, on a four-acre plot overlooking Six-mile Creek. In 1922 the facility was enlarged, and a private home was taken over as a nurses' residence. Later additions included a heating plant and laundry, and a wing for communicable diseases. This writer saw his first light of day in the hospital's maternity section in May of 1924, whereupon his proud father was presented with a bill for $73.10. Currently it is a domiciliary residence for older citizens.

THE NEW ELKS HOME. B. P. O. E. 636. ITHACA. N. Y.

This "new" home for Ithaca Lodge 636, Benevolent and Protective Order of Elks, constructed by Driscoll Brothers, opened on April 9, 1917. The land at State and Geneva Streets had been purchased in 1912 for $9,000; the total indebtedness of $70,000 was finally cleared at a mortgage-burning in 1943. The Ithaca Lodge was founded on 21 November, 1900, when a special train brought 100 sponsoring members from Auburn and Syracuse. They marched to the music of the Ithaca Band from the Lehigh depot to the Ithaca Hotel, where supper was served at 5 pm. "A real live goat was the prominent feature of the parade" according to the account of the festivities reported in the 50th. anniversary booklet issued by the Lodge five decades later. One can only assume that the lodge brothers were unsuccessful in securing the service of a "real live elk", for which a goat seems a poor substitute.

NEW MASONIC TEMPLE, ITHACA, N. Y.

The cornerstone of the Ithaca Masonic Temple was laid in September of 1925, and the building was officially opened and dedicated a year later. The Egyptian Revival structure was designed by the architectural firm of Gibb and Waltz and they provided space, as is traditional with Masonic Temples, for a small pipe organ — this one built by the famed H. P. Moller Company of Hagerstown, Maryland. Two lodges are associated with the temple: Fidelity Lodge #309 Free and Accepted Masons was first organized in Trumansburg in 1818; in 1846 it transferred to Ithaca and became Fidelity Lodge #51. Hobasco Lodge #716 F & AM was chartered in 1872. Each lodge currently has a membership of over 100.

4

Odd Fellows Temple, Ithaca, N.Y.

The Odd Fellows Temple was a mansion acquired from the J. C. Stowell estate in 1903 for $11,500; Stowell had been a wholesale grocer who started his business in 1835. Its parlors had magnificent chandeliers and fireplaces, and a pair of floor-to-ceiling framed mirrors which cost $485 — an enormous amount at the time the home was built. The building was constructed and first owned by Robert Halsey, an Odd Fellow; he sold it to the Stowells in 1861 for $6,500. Immediately after acquiring the building in 1903, the Odd Fellows constructed a 24-foot addition across the rear of the building, and rebuilt the attic into a sizable lodge room. An elaborate formal dedication was held on December 13, 1904. Membership peaked at 600, with more than 100 members commonly present at regular weekly meetings. The basement was later remodeled into a large banquet hall. The Tompkins County Public Library took over the property in 1966.

When the State Grand Lodge of the Odd Fellows planned a State Home and Orphanage, Mayor Louis P. Smith (an Odd Fellow himself and President of the Ithaca Gun Company) put forth a strenuous effort to have it located in the Ithaca area. What won over the site selection committee to the farm of Sidney D. Robertson on the Trumansburg Road was, according to *The Ithaca Journal*, "The wonderful view of Cayuga Lake, the city and Cornell University". The property was purchased for $14,000, and the buildings designed by Arthur N. Gibb and Ornan H. Waltz, probably the best-known local architects at the time. The buildings were constructed from stone taken from a quarry on the 120-acre site, with the work being done by the Ley Construction Company of Springfield, Illinois. The formal dedication was on May 14, 1923, and the Children's Home and Infirmary were dedicated on June 26. 1927.

INFIRMARY AT ODD FELLOWS STATE HOME

ORPHANAGE

ADMINISTRATION BUILDING AT ODD FELLOWS STATE HOME, ITHACA, N.Y.

The Ithaca branch of the Young Men's Christian Association was established in 1868. This fine brick structure, designed by Gibb and Waltz at the corner of Seneca and Buffalo Streets was built in 1898, and the youth of the community continued to be well served by it until Mother's Day, May of 1978, when it was totally destroyed by fire. Henry Abt chronicled the work of the YMCA in his famous 1926 book: "By establishing in the association's building facilities for bowling, pool, and other games, the YMCA in Ithaca has successfully combatted cheap bowling alleys and poolrooms, where bawdy thoughts and a low level of morals were once bred. The excellent gymnasium draws hundreds of young men to participate in clean and invigorating athletic competition." A new YMCA was built on Graham Road near the Pyramid Mall in the Town of Lansing, and as this book is written, over 2300 members benefit from the new facility. At the time of the fire, the old building was bursting at the seams to accomodate 1800 members.

Military and marching bands were very common in small towns in the later 1800's and early 1900's, and this group of musicians is pictured as they march past the new YMCA on Buffalo Street in 1908. The introduction of music education into the public schools, with the attendant development of bands and orchestras as part of their instructional programs, did much to eliminate the need for the traditional municipal band, and gradually they died out. Occasionally a clutch of interested musicians will form such a group, for nostalgic reasons if for no other, so today we are not entirely devoid of this type of music thanks to producers of records and tapes who have seen fit to preserve their efforts. There are many today who hold an especial appreciation for musical renditions played by bands like the one pictured here if their marching is smart and precise, the musicianship good, and particularly when our nation's flag is part of the display.

The Ithaca Fire Department, formally organized in 1871 from fifteen separate fire-fighting groups in the community, eventually offered protection by both professionals and volunteers. The air of pride in both meticulouly maintained equipment and a beautiful matched pair of dapple-gray horses is clearly evident on the faces of these men, as they indicate a high state of readiness to rush off to save valuable property and rescue beautiful women. Notice the kerosene lantern adjacent to the driver. The photograph was taken in front of the Cornell Library, which sided on Seneca Street, directly opposite the central fire station.

This is an excellent example of a "photo card", as contrasted with "commercially printed cards." Typically, a photo card was a scene captured by a local photographer who produced a small edition by printing them on special paper provided by Kodak and other firms, having on its back a space marked for a postage stamp, plus a dividing line for address and message. A commercial card was made in large quantities by printing presses and featured standard scenes. Photo cards, because of their rarity and special circumstances, command higher prices on today's collecting market. On this cold December day just before Christmas in 1917, a fire in an unidentified business has brought forth the hook and ladder wagon. Note the blankets on the horses, and the steering wheel or tiller at the rear of the wagon, an essential feature for getting around sharp corners. Readers can accept the challenge of determining the exact location of the scene!

On this Cayuga Street site was the Ithaca Academy, founded in 1823 as a private institution educating both males and females. In 1875 it became the Ithaca High School, under state legislation for public school systems. In September of 1885 construction of this high school was started. The first section cost $60,000 and, according to Henry Abt, "was considered too large for its purposes at that time." In 1893 and 1900 additions had to be built to accomodate the ever-increasing school-age population. Evidently the original planners were far-sighted in their thinking! The structure was destroyed by fire in 1912, as seen below.

One of Ithaca's most disasterous fires took place in the early morning hours of February 14, 1912, when the High School burned to the ground. The large central stair well in the school, a design prohibited by modern fire codes, created a chimney effect that made fighting the fire almost impossible. This rare photo card was distributed in black-and-white format, and also hand-tinted in red to indicate the lighting of the night-time sky by the fierce flames. Note the steam pumper. These powerful machines were capable of throwing immense quantities of water to great heights and long distances, but inevitably they gave way to pumps powered by the more easily-operated and managed internal combustion engines as the technology of gasoline powered equipment advanced in the early decades of the twentieth century.

High School, Ithaca, N. Y.

Ithaca High School, built to replace the one destroyed by fire, was designed to accomodate 1800 students. Driscoll Brothers was the contractor; C. J. Rumsey (of the hardware store) was the 'President' of the Building Committee of the Board of Education and Frank David Boynton was Superintendent of Schools. The famed William Henry Miller served as architect. In 1971, when the building was no longer to be used as a school, it was sold for a nominal sum for conversion to 'The DeWitt Mall' — a complex of stores, boutiques, and apartments — an eminently more satisfactory fate than the usual one of becoming a parking lot! Architect William Downing was responsible for the alterations. Note in this card how an artist has substituted a grassy plain for St. John's Episcopal Church, and how an out-of-perspective automobile has been faked into position on Seneca Street.

You'd never know it to look at this picture, but Cascadilla Street which runs on both sides of Casacadilla Creek as it makes its way through the flatlands of Ithaca is in the spring of the year a blaze of yellow. It's famous for its display of Forsythia, and in fact Ithaca almost seems to be a haven for this shrub. Indeed, Ithaca has been called The Forsythia City. This section of the city presents no particular problem for getting around after a snowfall, but the steep hillsides are an excellent training ground for automobile drivers of all ages. Long-time Ithaca residents are seldom intimidated by a bit of snow on a highway, unlike those whose experience in handling an automobile is limited to small amounts of the white stuff on level surfaces.

Rothschild Bros.' Department Store, Ithaca, N. Y.

Jacob Rothschild, an itinerant peddler who had immigrated from Poland at an early age, started his store in Ithaca in 1882. In 1889 when his brothers Daniel and Isaac joined him, he had become sufficiently successful that the business moved into the Wilgus Opera House building that we see here, at the corner of State and Tioga Streets. The Opera House was on the third and fourth floors, but eventually the store took over the entire building. The building immediately behind Rothschild's was the home of *The Ithaca Journal* from 1872 until 1905, when the store took over the property for expansion and *The Journal* moved to West State Street. Around 1914 the store was completely modernized, with new exterior walls. Rothschild Brothers Department Store lasted a full century; it closed in 1982.

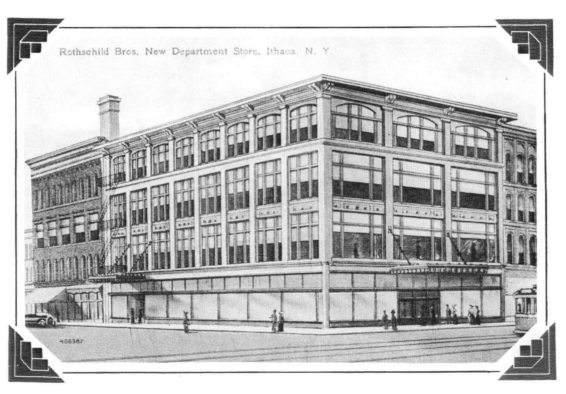

Rothschild Bros. New Department Store, Ithaca, N. Y.

Ithaca Savings Bank, Ithaca, N. Y.

The Ithaca Savings Bank, currently known as the Citizen's Savings Bank, traces its history back to 1868. It took over this site at the corner of Tioga and Seneca Streets in 1878, and William H. Miller designed the bank building, which opened in 1887 to replace a private dwelling that had at one time been the home of Ezra Cornell's son Alonzo. In 1921 that building burned, and architects Gibb and Waltz designed the structure seen here which went into service in 1924. Recently the space between the two towers has been filled, and a giant four-story bay-window now faces Seneca Street where a void is seen in this view. The building immediately to the left is the Tompkins County Trust Company. The well-known Seneca Building appeared in 1928, just beyond the far side of the bank on Seneca Street. One of the lesser-known of the many practical jokes perpetrated by the late Hugh Troy involved The Ithaca Savings Bank. He picked up from the countryside a large "JESUS SAVES" sign and one night erected it on the building facade, for all the passers-by to see the following morning. It is said that the officials of the bank were not amused.

The primary reason for including this picture is to show the Office Hotel, on the southwest corner of State and Cayuga Streets. A simple building, it was for many years one of the lesser establishments on State street and was, in the eyes of many, something in the nature of a flophouse. This may be an unfair characterization, but nevertheless it was a common impression particularly by those who never had occasion to frequent the place. It came down in the mid-1940's to make way for the Chanticleer, a restaurant and watering place. The scene pre-dates 1921, when the Treman, King building on the southeast corner of this intersection was destroyed by fire, to be replaced by a structure designed by Arthur N. Gibb and Ornan H. Waltz. Note the stately columns of the Clinton House (see the back cover) on the right, and the marquee of the Lyceum Theatre at the rear left.

North Cayuga Street Looking South   Ithaca, N. Y.

Interior Lyceum Theatre.   Ithaca, N. Y.

The Lyceum Theatre, located on Cayuga Street next to the Jamieson-McKinney building, opened for business in 1893 and continued until around 1924. Its auditorium was parallel to Cayuga Street, behind the two buildings to its south. Notice the fancy loges and the general theme of elaborate decor. The piano in the orchestra pit suggests that the many silent movies were accompanied by a musician expert in the art of playing themes appropriate to whatever scene appeared on the silver screen. For many years it was used by the Ithaca Conservatory of Music (now Ithaca College) as an auditorium. The Lyceum's interior makes an interesting study in the architectural styling of the day. Note particularly the interesting arrangement of the aisle; no doubt the architect had some pet theory that this would maximize sight lines for the greatest number of patrons. Other Ithaca theatres were the "Happy Hour" —a nickelodeon—in the Cornell Library Building, and the Star, built in 1911 on Seneca Street opposite today's Seneca Building, and the still-standing Crescent built on Aurora Street in 1915. After their theatre usefulness ended, both the Star and the Crescent served as gymnasiums for Ithaca College. The Strand on East State Street was built in 1917, while the State was erected in 1928 — an excellent example of a 1920-style movie palace, with ornate plaster work, a cloud machine projecting cumulus images across the starry ceiling, and a 3-manual Link Theatre Pipe Organ with all the drums and traps associated with this class of instrument. The organ was made in near-by Binghamton; Edwin A. Link, its installer and son of the builder, gained fame as the inventor of the Link aviation flight trainer so important to the Allied cause in training pilots to help win World War II. The Temple Theatre on Seneca Street featured serials and grade B movies and westerns. The Ithaca Theatre on West State Street was built in the late 1930's.

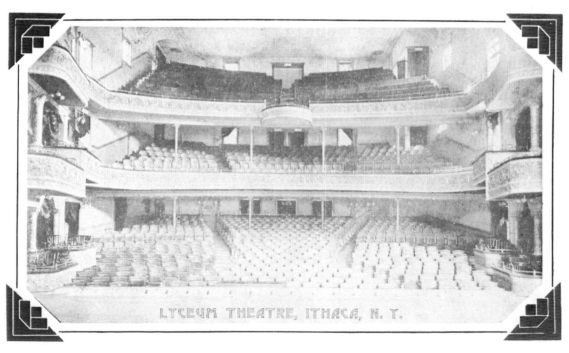

LYCEUM THEATRE, ITHACA, N. Y.

The Cornell Infirmary.   Ithaca, N. Y.

Henry W. Sage, who had conducted his business career in Brooklyn, New York, retired at the age of sixty-six in 1877 and moved to Ithaca where he engaged William H. Miller to design the fine mansion seen here on East State Street. After his death in 1897 his sons gave the home to Cornell for use as an infirmary, together with an endowment for its upkeep. The structure at the far left is a later addition to the university's medical facility, a very plain building obviously built with economy in mind.

Built in 1866 by George McChain on land bought from Ezra Cornell, this fine old Italianate townhouse was sold in 1884 to Douglass Boardman, first Dean of the Cornell University Law School and a prominent lawyer and judge. Boardman died in 1891 just before the founding of the Ithaca Conservatory of Music, chartered as Ithaca College in 1932. When Mrs. Boardman died in 1910, the Conservatory acquired the house, which later served the college as music department headquarters, administration building, and art museum. [Tompkins County Trust Company Landmark Series] Only by heroic efforts on the part of preservation-minded citizens during the 1970's was this historic house saved for future generations.

Ithaca Conservatory of Music, Ithaca, N. Y.

13

Simeon DeWitt was born in 1756 in Ulster County, and he attended Rutgers University for two years. In 1777 he joined the patriot army, where he became a surveyor and geographer. He eventually became surveyor general under George Washington. After the Revolutionary War DeWitt was appointed surveyor general of New York State; he became interested in Cayuga Lake property and purchased most of what is now Ithaca. It was he who gave the community its name. The park which bears his name is a lovely and relaxing place which

DE WITT PARK, SHOWING CONSERVATORY OF MUSIC, ITHACA, N. Y.

provided the equivalent of a campus quadrangle for Ithaca College while it was located downtown. Note that in this view the central tower of St. Paul's Methodist Church is still in place, and the space between the college's Little Theatre and the Baptist Church to the north is vacant. Boardman House is at the right, and the Presbyterian Church and the County Court House are behind the trees at the left.

Patrick Conway, who died in 1929, came to Ithaca in 1895 to assume leadership of the Ithaca Band at a time when almost every community across America had an organized music group of this nature. Unlike most early town bands, however, Patsy Conway engaged top-flight musicians to perform, so that his ensemble was comparable to some of the finest bands in the country, such as those headed by John Philip Sousa and Arthur Pryor. It became much more than just a local band, and made tours all over the country just as leading symphony orchestras do today. The band made many recordings in the early days of the phonograph industry; today Edison cylinder records of the Conway Band (which is the name by which it became best-known) are highly prized collector's items. In 1922 the Conway Band School was organized as an affiliate of the Ithaca Conservatory of Music (now Ithaca College); eventually Ithaca College became one of the best-known schools in the United States for training musicians anxious to teach music in the public schools.

ITHACA BAND
PATRICK CONWAY, CONDUCTOR

The Moving Picture World of September 13, 1913, tells us that Ithaca's first Star Theatre was at the corner of Tioga and Green Streets, opening in 1908, and was supplanted by this new Star which opened on September 13, 1911. It had a seating capacity of 1,200 and every chair was upholstered in genuine leather, at a cost of $7 per chair. During the regular theatrical season two acts of vaudeville were used in conjunction with the pictures, and a five-piece orchestra, under the able direction of Professor J. A. Noble, "put the finishing touches to a

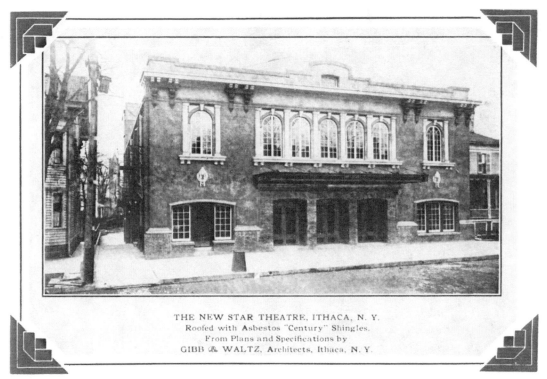

THE NEW STAR THEATRE, ITHACA, N. Y.
Roofed with Asbestos "Century" Shingles.
From Plans and Specifications by
GIBB & WALTZ, Architects, Ithaca, N. Y.

well-selected program." The building itself was constructed of hollow tile and concrete, faced with plaster and trimmed in white (and, as noted on this advertising post-card, the roof was made of Asbestos 'Century' shingles). $50,000 was invested in the Star by the Star Theatre Stock Company, consisting of Fred B. Howe, President and General Manager; John B. Howe, Secretary and Treasurer; F. W. Grant, Vice-President; and Charles L. Hamer, Business Manager. Fred Howe and Charles Hamer were old-time vaudeville musicians with a long record in the amusement business. The Howe brothers conducted "a prominent dental business" in Ithaca apart from their theatrical interests. Ithaca College took over the building for a gymnasium in the early 1920's, and thereafter it was known as the Seneca Gymnasium.

Ithaca College, Administration and Little Theatre Buildings, Ithaca, N. Y.

Probably no institution in America has offered more in the way of higher education, based on less investment in physical plant and financial endowment, than has Ithaca College. It was founded by William Grant Egbert in 1892 as the Ithaca Conservatory of Music in which stock was sold, apparently with the idea that it could not only dispense education, but make a profit at the same time, a notion soon abandoned. By the 1930's Ithaca College had become widely known for excellence in the fields of Music, Physical Education, and Drama, and it conducted classes and did its work in a miscellaneous array of buildings all over downtown Ithaca. The Little Theatre building fronted on DeWitt Park, as did the band building at the left, and various administrative functions were carried out in the Boardman House which joined the theatre building, to the right. Eventually the task of continuing to operate a first-class institution in this environment was deemed impracticable, and thanks to generous Federal loan monies, the campus on South Hill was developed in the 1950's and 1960's. Ithaca College has now widely diversified into such fields as Physical Therapy, Radio and Television, Arts and Sciences, and Business.

Copyright 1906 by the Corner Book Stores.
Congregational Church, Ithaca, N. Y.

Har

Your author was raised in this church when it was the First Congregational Church, and for many hours he gazed, seated in padded pews, at the Lord's Prayer and the 23rd. Psalm featured on the panels at the right and the left of the apse. The structure was designed by William Henry Miller, the architect of so many Victorian-era structures including the Cornell library. Some might even suggest a resemblance between this church's steeple and the library tower, the famed spire that has become the Univeristy's hallmark. This building was built in 1884, and incorporated at least two windows by Louis Comfort Tiffany. Remodeling took place in the early 1920's, and in 1959 the Congregationalists built a new church in Cayuga Heights, with Ithaca College's music department taking over this building. In 1966 St. Catherine's Greek Orthodox Church assumed ownership. Note the gas lights in the interior view of the sanctuary in its original configuration. Both of these cards were printed in Germany.

Interior-Congregational Church.   Ithaca, N. Y.

Church of the
Immaculate Conception.
Ithaca, N. Y.

Catholocism has been an important part of the Ithaca scene since the 1830's; the Reverend Peter Connolly of Auburn celebrated Holy Mass for the first time here in 1837, in a private home. The first resident pastor, a Father Guilbride, served two years after 1848, and in 1850 the first church—on the site of the present rectory—came into being in what apparently had been a residence. The second church, located on the site of the present edifice, was dedicated in 1860. In 1895 the growing parish started a subscription drive and $17,000 was raised to use toward a much-needed new and larger structure, which was designed by A. B. Wood of Ithaca, and built by John Dempsey of Elmira under a contract bid of $49,877.77. It was dedicated by Bishop Bernard McQuaid on September 11, 1898, and according to the *Ithaca Daily Journal* in its description of this happy occasion, "Protestants formed at least one-third of the crowd of at least eighteen hundred people inside the four walls of the church." The debt was finally cleared in January, 1947, as announced by Reverend William Byrne, who served many years as pastor after 1928.

In 1912, the parishioners gave Father William Harrington, then their pastor, a gift of $6,712.73 which he promptly used to purchase a pipe organ which was subsequently dedicated at a recital by Professor Eugene Bonn, organist of St. Patrick's Cathedral in Rochester. The sanctuary of Ithaca's Church of the Immaculate Conception was remodeled in the 1930's, and the new main altar was provided from a bequest in the will of Mrs. Mary E. Collins. The side altars were given by Mr. and Mrs. Frank Speno. Speno developed what bacame a worldwide business little-known to most Ithacans. He came to America at the age of 13, a penniless immigrant from Italy, and went to work as a laborer for the Lackawanna Railroad. He became a foreman, and eventually conceived the idea of a big machine which would clean the ballast underneath the tracks. He was able to get engineers to design and build the machine, and it and others like it were soon used all over America, and eventually around the world. Speno Rail Services had its offices for many years on South Cayuga Street, until the company was sold around 1977, at which time its headquarters was moved to Syracuse.

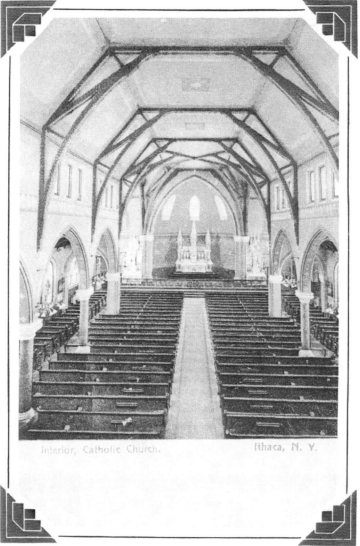

Interior, Catholic Church.   Ithaca, N. Y.

Presbyterian Church, Ithica, N.Y.

This structure went into service in 1901, at a cost of $130,843.96 according to a report in the church's 100th. anniversary history, published in 1904 (the most recent history of the church to date). J. Cleveland Cady of New York City was the architect, and Thomas B. Campbell was the builder. 233 persons made gifts totalling some $59,000 towards construction, and only $28,000 of debt remained when the building was opened. By 1905 this was reduced to $14,000. The Presbyterians have always represented a substantial proportion of the protestant church community in Ithaca, and at this writing have some 1300 individual members. The sanctuary is the largest in the city.

First Baptist Church, Ithaca, N.Y.

The design work of William H. Miller evidences itself once again in the third Baptist church to occupy this site on the edge of DeWitt Park. The first opened in 1831, the second was completed in 1855, and this structure was completed in 1880. The Standard Oil magnate John D. Rockefeller, who was born in near-by Richford and was generous in his support of Baptist causes, gave $12,000 towards the construction cost of $30,000.

First Methodist Church. Ithaca, N. Y.

This structure was designed by architects Brown and Davis of Chicago and Cincinnati, and was dedicated in 1909 as the Methodist Episcopal Church. The central tower had long been removed when the congregation merged with the State Street Methodist Church in 1960, to become St. Paul's United Methodist Church. The church's first organ was built by the short-lived Hope-Jones Organ Company of Elmira, in which Mark Twain was an investor. Robert Hope-Jones was a British-born electrical wizard who developed what became known as the Hope-Jones Unit Orchestra, a pipe organ that could simulate an entire orchestra, designed for accompanying the films of the expanding silent movie industry. He soon ran his Elmira business into bankruptcy, whereupon it was taken over by the Rudolph Wurlitzer Company in North Tonawanda, New York, which wanted the Hope-Jones' expertise in spite of their knowledge of his prior business failures. The result of their short-lived union (Hope-Jones committed suicide soon thereafter) was "The Mighty Wurlitzer"—the famed pipe organ which graced the majority of the great movie palaces of the 1920's.

State Street, M. E. Church   Ithaca, N. Y.

The church in this scene, complete with its lofty steeple, was built in 1879 at the corner of Albany and State Streets where the Salvation Army now holds forth. Methodism has a long and interesting history in the city. This church is an outgrowth of the Methodist Church on Aurora Street, but only after first having had a structure on Seneca and Plain Streets. The steeple suffered the same fate as many other church spires, damage by lightning and storm—so it was removed many years before the edifice itself was demolished in 1961 when structural weaknesses revealed safety hazards. At this time the two Methodist groups were re-united, under the name St. Paul's United Methodist Church. Carol Kammen, writing in the Ithaca Journal in 1983, tells us that in 1913 the auditorium was spruced up and a new organ was installed, with Andrew Carnegie contributing $1,500 towards its cost, said instrument going to the Homer Avenue Church in Cortland when the building was demolished. Some of the pews went to the Methodist Church in Varick; others went to Ithaca's Greek Orthodox Church just down the street. Incidental items went to churches in Kennedy's Corner, Enfield, Ellis Hollow, and West Danby.

First Unitarian Church, Ithaca, N. Y.

The First Unitarian Society was organized in 1865, the same year that Cornell University was chartered, and indeed, Ezra Cornell was a regular attendant at services. William Henry Miller, the famed local architect who conveniently happened to be a Unitarian, designed this building; it was dedicated in 1869, and cost $26,000 plus $7,000 for the land. Mr. Miller's services were donated in memory of his mother, according to information in the booklet "A Century of Unitarian History in Ithaca", published in 1965.

This placid scene of 'The Twelve Apostles' from four generations back hardly suggests that Meadow Street would someday be a busy artery, with cars and trucks bustling to and fro where only horse and buggy traffic appears in this picture. The neat row of houses were the treasured homes of working men and women of the time, and the new sidewalks are a sign that prosperity reigned. The steep slopes of State and Mitchell Streets and Ithaca Road where Route 13 ran for many years were frequently the scene of bad accidents as trucks got heavier and larger, as on occasion brakes proved insufficient for holding them to manageable speeds on the downgrade. In order to minimize this carnage, Route 13 was re-routed after World War II through the Town of Lansing on a wide sweep north of Ithaca and Cayuga Heights, on a gentler slope above the east shore of Cayuga Lake, offering a much safer approach to the city's populated areas. Within the city limits, Meadow Street assumes this burden as Route 13 wends its way to the southwest and, eventually, Elmira.

Meadow St.   Ithaca, N.Y.

Copyright 1905 by the Rotograph Co.

5180 E. State Street, Ithaca, N. Y.

Imagine — State Street without any automobiles! Note the Post Office in the Colonial Building, at the right. In 1905, when the Rotograph Company copyrighted this card, cars were just beginning to make an appearance, and Henry Ford had been in business for just two years . . . but the ubiquitous Model T had yet to appear, and there was a little time left before the famous "flivvers" and other makes filled the streets of Ithaca and everywhere else in the United States to create monstrous traffic jams. In Ithaca's case, eventually the powers-that-be simply said "Enough!" and banished cars to side streets, to create "The Commons", the pedestrian walk-way that now occupies this entire scene. In a sense, we're now closer to 1905.

Can anything possibly surpass memories of the circus? Lucky indeed are those whose parents took them as small children early in a morning to watch the show being unloaded from the circus train, usually at the DL & W tracks, and to see the "big top" being erected—most likely at the fair grounds on Meadow Street. Elephants helping to raise the giant poles; roustabouts swinging in unison to drive the tent stakes; cooks organizing food in the meal tent for scores of performers and workers — the circus was always a little World of its own, amazing for outsiders to see. Once everything was in place, the parade followed State Street — and every onlooker had his or her favorite sight. Whether it was the ponderous pachyderms in single file, the pretty ladies on horseback, the animals pacing in their cages, the band perched high on the top of the band wagon, or perhaps the last thing in the parade always the incredibly loud steam calliope—all served to take Ithacans for a brief trip to fantasy-land. The smells, the excitement, the noise of the parade—all were intended to draw patrons to the afternoon or evening show, after which the circus was packed up and moved to another town where the whole process was repeated. This postcard by photographer John Troy was postmarked in 1908.

This handsome Greek revival structure with its classic Ionic columns dates back to 1830, when it served as the Bank of Ithaca. In 1882 the Post Office moved in and stayed until its new home on Tioga Street became available, after which the Atwater grocery occupied it. Mr. Atwater added the side-structures, and this is the way it appeared ca. 1915. The Knights of Columbus has the second story, and the Martin Dance Studio the third. On both outer columns appear ads for Heinz Cider Vinegar and playbills for the Lyceum Theatre; the left one features both Mary Pickford and Charlie Chaplin. Ads on the center columns promote Park & Tilford's Chocolate and Bon-Bons, as well as Herbert L. Cobb, a dealer who sold DL & W Coal and hard and soft woods. Between the center columns is a large "Fresh Fish" sign. Krum's News Room and Cigar Store at the right featured a Shoe Shine Parlor, and above it Underwood Typewriters were sold with a big sign proclaiming "Underwood Wins Grand Prize — Panama Pacific Exhibition — Highest Award for Typewriting." In later years the Fanny Farmer candy store was where Krum's is shown, and the miniature blinking beacon inside its store-front window was a familiar sight to Ithacans for years. In the 1930's the main store-front was extended outward, at the expense of the bottom portion of the two center columns.

The grocery store founded by Fred Atwater in 1886 was for many years an Ithaca landmark, here seen in its prominent downtown position in the Colonial Building at 109 East State Street where it remained until 1952. This neatly organized operation is cited as "Atwater's Cash Grocery and Bakery," a reflection of the fact that in those days many grocery stores carried customers on a credit basis, which inevitably meant higher costs for everyone, a situation Mr. Atwater apparently wished to avoid. Notice the columns surrounded with carefully placed boxes and cans of packaged goods. Your writer recalls that in 1941, as Business Manager of the Ithaca High School yearbook, the store manager would not okay a proof of their advertisement until it was returned with the apostrophe removed before the s at the end of the name, yet on this card and in the picture of the Colonial Building elsewhere in this book the apostrophe is clearly evident. We're confused.

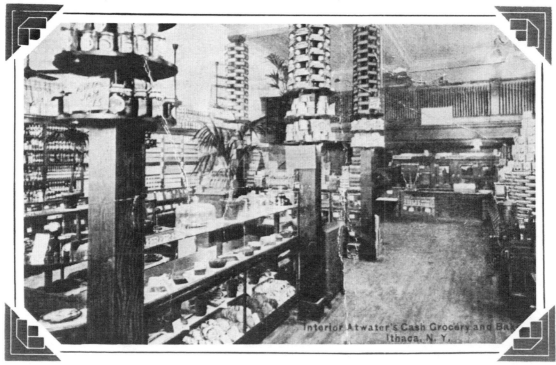

Interior Atwater's Cash Grocery and Bakery
Ithaca, N. Y.

In a day when our streets are jammed with cars and trucks and air pollution is a matter of concern, it's tempting to think that maybe we would be better off with horse-drawn vehicles such as these which were all over Ithaca in the early days of this century. Everyone likes horses, of course, but the fact is that they don't come equipped with catalytic convertors and they provide plenty of their own brand of pollution which was, in its day, a major source of disease and pestilence even though the city spent plenty of money for street cleaners equipped with brooms, shovels, and push-carts to clean up after the animals. One of Ithaca's major retailers of coal for household fuel was the East Hill Coal Yards on Maple Avenue, and it relied on horses for delivery work until its big shed burned in the early 1930's. Its location was such that almost all deliveries were to lower altitudes throughout the city, and to get down the steep grades with some degree of safety, brake blocks were often set under the wagon wheels. The steel bottoms of these blocks made well-remembered showers of sparks as the animals tugged the heavy wagons down such grades as Ithaca Road which, by that date, was paved with concrete.

Scenes of State Street abound in this book, but none seem quite so quaint to some observers in the later years of the 20th century as this one. The town's major hotel was then The 'New' Ithaca, traffic lights were off in the future, horses hauled wagons on any side of the street their driver pleased, and trolleys were an important means of conducting the commerce of the city. Notice the many canvas awnings, so important for keeping rooms reasonably cool in those hot summer pre-air-conditioned times, and in the basement corner of the Ithaca Hotel the barber shop which was a fixture for generations.

The four-story brick Ithaca Hotel was for many years a prominent building on the southwest corner of State and Aurora Streets. The structure was opened in 1872 to architect Alfred B. Dale's designs to accomodate 200 guests. The walls came tumbling down 95 years later in 1967 to make way for "urban renewal." Every community needs the services of a good hostelry, and over its long existence the Ithaca Hotel provided these in good measure. In its place the Iszard Department Store was erected. The first Ithaca Hotel was on the same spot, a frame building erected in 1809; it was destroyed by fire in 1871. Note the attractive (for its day) 'sleeping apartment' and the 'parlor', with their 'busy' wallpaper and ornately patterned carpet so characteristic of the late- Victorian period, as seen below.

ITHACA HOTEL, INTERIOR

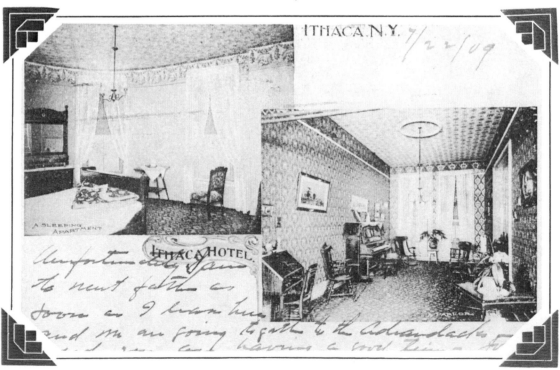

FAMOUS "DUTCH KITCHEN"—ITHACA HOTEL, ITHACA, N. Y.

The Dutch Kitchen, a favorite Tompkins County watering hole, was an important feature of the Ithaca Hotel. The heavy wood furniture almost invited diners and drinkers to carve their names and initials so that future patrons might know what distinguished guests had proceeded them, and by the time the place was demolished, carving and whittling had taken place on almost every square inch of surface in the room! An earlier postcard, handled by the post office in 1907, refers to The Dutch Kitchen as "one of the most noted student resorts in the country."

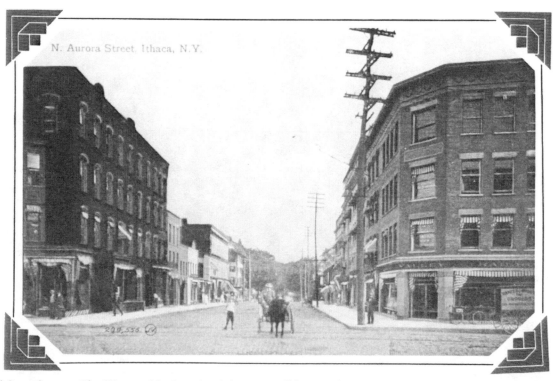

N. Aurora Street, Ithaca, N.Y.

Aurora and State Streets: The Wanzer block at the right was well known for many years to travelers, as the Lehigh Valley Railroad ticket office occupied the ground floor corner, thus saving them the necessity of going to the far end of the city to arrange for accomodations to hither and yon via the iron horse. Just beyond the ticket office was the Wanzer grocery, and beyond that, Head's Camera Shop which for many years was the photographic headquarters for Ithacans. During the late 1920's and early 1930's Mr. Wanzer had a delivery truck which was the equivalent of what we today call a van, but with screened open sides, and fabric curtains for inclement weather. It had a cadet visor over the windshield that had painted on it "HERE COMES WANZER" and on the tail gate was its counterpart "THERE GOES WANZER."

Brill-made car #27, ordered in 1903, is similar to car #31 seen elsewhere in this book. It's on its way to Eddy Street as it rumbles past Merrill's Corner Pharmacy and the C. W. Freeman Tin Shop. Next to the drug store, on South Aurora Street, we see Aaron Wells' High Grade Second Hand Clothing emporium, and then a restaurant with a board in front advertising 'Regular Meals and Quick Lunches—Chops and Steaks of All Kinds—Oysters in Season — Sandwiches', followed by the Hub Hotel. For years the Western Union Telegraph Office was located at No. 105, and it was easily recognized by the admonition on its front window "Don't Write, Telegraph". The Aurora Street hill has always been a hazard to traffic, and periodically a runaway vehicle comes tearing down the slope, threatening life and limb of anyone in its path. The city and the state try hard, not always successfully, to get heavy trucks and vehicles to use alternate routes into the city.

This 1906 view down Buffalo Street, which was hand-colored in its original form, cannot help but be somewhat misleading to one not familiar with Ithaca's topography. The block between Eddy Street, where the photograph was taken, and Stewart Avenue—crossing half way down in the distance—is very steep indeed, even if it doesn't look that way in the picture. In the winters of years past, young residents of East Hill who walked down this grade on frigid mornings to attend Ithaca High School frequently enjoyed estab-

East Buffalo Str. looking down from top of Hill, Ithaca, N. Y.

lishing great slides down the snowy and icy sidewalks. Conversely, motorists trying to make the upgrade had their work cut out for them. Before it became common practice for city crews to spread salt for melting and abrasives such as sand or cinders on the streets to offer a modicum of traction, motorists were obliged to use chains on their wheels. Your writer spent many hours, as a young gas-station attendant, grumbling and saying bad words as he struggled to fit them to the vehicles of customers who rushed in for this service as the white stuff started to accumulate. Notice the interesting lighting fixture on the left, probably gas-illuminated.

Every city has its 'hub', and Ithaca's has always been the corner of State and Tioga Streets. For many years the chronicler of goings on about town was Romeyn Berry, a lawyer, writer, and manager of the Cornell University Athletic Association, through his regular column 'State and Tioga' which appeared in *The Ithaca Journal* — indicating the importance of this spot in the hearts and minds of the townspeople. Today it is the 'hub' of the Ithaca Commons, formed by making a pedestrian mall of State Street from Aurora to Cayuga, and of Tioga Street from State to Seneca. At the time of this picture, from this spot one could ride the trolley northward on Tioga and make connections all the way to Auburn, and thence to much of the rest of the eastern United States via the great network of Interurban Electric Railways that existed for a brief period in the early 20th. Century.

Ezra Cornell made his money in the telegraph business, and he elected to use his fortune for the benefit of mankind, rather than exclusively for his own family. His first major civic philanthropy was the gift to Ithaca of the Cornell Library, as seen on the left. The library proper was on the second floor; the first floor served as a bank, and the lower level was 'Library Hall' which was used for various meetings and in later years as a theatre. The impressive brick building at the right is the Ithaca Savings Bank, built in 1887 to designs of William H. Miller. Adjoining it, against the first stone arch, is the Masonic Block, which had a masonic hall on the fourth floor. As a child your writer was frequently taken to the Cornell Library by his father, who succeeded in developing in his son a love of books. The memories of taking out *Aesop's Fables*, Hamlin Garland's *Boy Life On the Prairie*, Wallace Wadsworth's version of *Tales of Paul Bunyan* and other similar works to be read and re- read in his Oxford Place home in East Hill's Bryant Tract are vivid indeed.

North Geneva Str, from Corner West Seneca, Ithaca, N. Y.

The "Three Grey Ladies", a magnificent grouping of classic Greek revival homes is seen on the west side of North Geneva Street. In the first block north of Seneca Street once stood these three examples of Corinthian, Ionic, and Doric architectural styles. As this book is written, the second and third remain, the first a victim of "economic progress," to make way for a gas station. Preservationists who see such structures as an important link to the past view such "progress" at best as a civic tragedy; at worst, a civic atrocity.

Such a peaceful scene! In a day when automobiles overflow everywhere and there just doesn't seem to be enough parking space no matter what civic planners and authorities do to try to keep up with the output of the car makers' factories, it's refreshing to look back at a time when life was seemingly less hectic. North Geneva Street in the early part of the 20th Century was typical of neighborhoods everywhere across America, with about the only noise being produced during the day coming from the clip-clop of horse's hooves pulling an occasional wagon on the brick pavement. Ithaca is misspelled "Ithica" on this and many other post cards, many of which were printed in Germany prior to World War I.

N. Geneva Street Ithica N.Y.

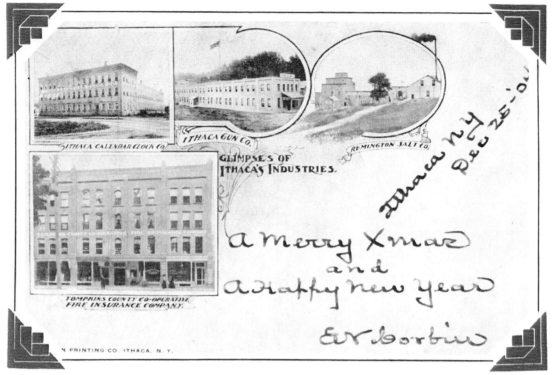

Aside from Cornell, no product of local concerns did more to spread the name Ithaca around the world in the late 1800's than did the Ithaca Calendar Clock Company. The company made clocks with at least fifteen different languages printed on their dials, including Spanish, Portuguese, French, German, Russian, and Turkish in addition to English. J. H. Haws invented his calendar mechanism in 1853, and in 1854 W. H. Akins and J. C. Burritt scored a major coup when they figured out a way to make the clock put an extra day in February every fourth year. This was a great sales gimmick, and helped build the company to the point where in 1875 sixty men were producing 30 clocks per day. Henry B. Horton, another inventive genius, was a major factor in the success of the business. He also developed a line of automatic musical instruments — small paper-roll-music and wooden pinned-cylinder-operated table-top reed organs produced under the name of The Autophone Company. These were sold in very large numbers, with Sears & Roebuck and Montgomery Ward featuring them in their catalogs for years. The business went bankrupt in 1920. Today Ithaca Calendar Clocks and the music machines, such as the Autophone, the Gem and Concert roller organs are highly collected items.

For many years after its 1880 founding, Ithaca shotguns were considered by sportsmen to be about the finest available. Three generations of the Smith family (following in the footsteps of founder LeRoy H. Smith) made certain that their product was not only of superior quality, but that their dealers could sell them profitably. By 1926 there were 350 employees at the Lake Street plant. During World War II .45 calibre automatic pistols were made, as many as 20,000 per month during peak production. In the 1960's the firm was sold to a business conglomerate, which tried to increase sales by selling through discount houses, which promptly destroyed the fine relationships with retailers that had been developed over many years. To meet the sales that the new owners thought would be forthcoming, production was increased, to the detriment of quality. The result was a predictable disaster, and the proud Ithaca Gun Company closed. As this book is written, a locally-financed group has re-opened the shop and former employees are working hard to re-establish the business, by reverting to the time-honored principles of producing nothing but the best, and reorganizing the sales strategies. In its early days the company also made typewriters.

In 1915 the Thomas Brothers Aircraft Company of Bath, New York, merged with the Morse Chain Company in Ithaca to form the Thomas-Morse Aircraft Company. The Thomas-Morse "Scout", of which 600 were built in the factories on South Hill, though a successful scouting and trainer craft of the era never saw combat service during World War I. After the war the company designed the very successful Model MB-3, and built 50 of them for the government. Then the Army put a production contract for another 200 out to bid, and this was won by a bid of $1,448,000, $127,000 lower than the Ithaca firm's price, by a fledgling outfit in Seattle, Washington, headed by lumber dealer tycoon William Boeing. It has been suggested that the ready availability of spruce (it being the basic construction material for airplanes in those days) in the Pacific northwest, was the reason for Boeing's low bid. By 1922 Boeing was in the black, and it is fair to suggest that the Ithaca design was largely responsible for getting Boeing into the airplane business in a big way. Thomas-Morse eventually was merged into the Consolidated Aircraft Corporation. The post card view shows a Thomas-Morse "Scout" in service with the U. S. Army in Texas.

Lt. T. G. Ellyson was the first naval officer trained to fly, and he was instructed by Glenn Curtiss who also built the craft at Hammondsport, New York. *The Ithaca Daily Journal* waxed eloquent about his flight over Ithaca, which took place in connection with the Tompkins County Fair: "Birdman Thrice Soars O'er Track and Fields — Lt. T. G. Ellyson, The Curtis Aviator, Treats Tompkins County Citizens to the Most Successful Aerial Maneuvers Ever Seen in This Part of the State —Sails Over West Hill Amid Cheers of Record Crowd on the County Fair Grounds — Flight Over South Hill Scheduled for Today. . . Ellyson followed the ground for a distance of about 100 feet, then tilted his planes and arose gracefully like a huge bird. His machine rode beautifully under his skillful manipulations and there were exclamations of delight from the crowd as the wonderful exhibition. . . Over six-mile creek he turned and soared with a beautiful dip over his hangar and touching the field a few yards from where he started, shut off his engine and glided about 100 yards, amid the applause of the crowd and tooting of automobile horns and whistles. It was the first flight ever made in the City of Ithaca and was a truly beautiful one." It must have been an exciting day in the home town.

Richard Kerr, the chronicler of Ithaca's Street Railway system, tells us that car 31, a single-truck 30-foot 7-window design, was built by Brill of Philadelphia in 1906 and was acquired for use in Ithaca on the Cayuga Heights lines, c. 1910. Within the confines of its 105-inch width and 18' 10" body it had crosswise seating for 28 passengers; it was powered by two General Electric motors. The body color was green, with light cream on the lower side panels and all sash areas, and the lettering was gold. The company employees have adopted a serious mien for the photographer, and it is not clear if they are a motorman-conductor team, of if one is just along for the ride. To have two men handling a small car like this would have been most unusual, even in those days of low-cost labor.

This car, proceeding east in this pre-1912 picture past the Rothschild Store on the south side of State Street toward the corner of Tioga, appears to be one of the Cayuga Heights trolleys, to judge by its overall design. As in the case of main-line railroads, there were seemingly endless reorganizations and bankruptcies of the various firms that made up the city's public transportation system, and The Cayuga Heights Railway was one of them. Note The Corner Book Store at the right, a business still very much in operation. For many years it was on Tioga Street; currently it holds forth on Cayuga Street.

Again, according to Richard Kerr's fascinating book *The Ithaca Street Railway*, this scene depicts "a very popular postcard photo of car 14 heading off Eddy Street at Dryden Road, onto a section of private right-of-way. The White Memorial Entrance [to the Cornell Campus], or 'Andy's Chocolate Cake', and Cayuga Lake are visible in this view from the 1890's." The private section of track ran past Cascadilla Hall. The gateway, of alternate layers of white sandstone and reddish brown limestone, was built in 1896 with funds provided by former President White, and its color scheme is the basis for the chocolate-cake moniker. Ever since the dawn of the automobile age, its narrow passage has been an aggravation to motorists.

In 1911, when this card passed through the post office, trolley cars were very much a part of the Ithaca and Cornell scene. Residents of the south side of Cascadilla Hall, and most especially those who had the bay windows at their disposal, had a fine view of the cars as they rumbled up and down the private right-of-way of the trolley company adjacent to the building. At the right is Dryden Road where it joins Eddy Street.

In 1906 a ten-mile loop of trolley-car track was completed which went through what is now Cayuga Heights, to descend the hill near what is today Remington Road, and on to Renwick Park—now Stewart Park. This curve is at the northern end of the short-lived loop, which operated for only a couple of years. Note the boat pier extending from Renwick Park into the lake.

With the sparcity of population along the outer loop of the trolley line, is it any wonder that service lasted for only two years? It was a beautiful trip, especially in an open car like this one on a fine summer's day, but private business cannot exist on sentiment nor the occasional patron who takes a ride just for the view.

Trolleys were always popular pictures for postcards. In this 1904 scene a car of the Ithaca Street Railway makes its way around "Lookout Point" on The Knoll above the junction of Thurston Avenue and Cayuga Heights Road. The "Outer Loop", of which this section of track was a part, went into operation in May of 1900.

The trolley bridge over Cascadilla Creek, just north of Collegetown, looks like a spindly affair. However, such structures didn't have to be as rugged as bridges we see today. Only one car at a time was ever on the bridge; trolley cars are relatively light, and they don't set up dynamic loading conditions as do steam engines. In those days bridge designers didn't have to concern themselves with excess steelwork to counter the destructive effects of salt as today's engineers are obliged to do. After the last trolley ran on the 22nd. of June, 1935, the bridge was given a floor and guardrails, and served as a pedestrian footbridge for a number of years.

Ithaca, N.Y.
at House near Inlet.

This lovely view suggests a beautiful sylvan glade, and the lands around the inlet to Cayuga Lake have always been a favorite spot for boaters. The city dump for many years was adjacent to this scene, however, and it wasn't until the 1930's under a WPA Project that the disposal site was turned into a public golf course. Before the advent of the railroads, Cayuga Lake was an important artery of commerce, particularly for coal from the Pennsylvania mines brought overland from the Susquehanna River on the Ithaca-Owego Railroad (initially horse-drawn) then moved northward on barges and boats to the Erie Canal. Today the use of the inlet is primarily recreational, with many yachts and sailboats harbored at numerous anchorages and boat houses.

JOHNSONS BOAT HOUSE

C. B. PORTER

CAYUGA INLET IN FEBRUARY   122039

Fred E. Johnson started his boat yards around 1908, and at one time he controlled properties all along Cascadilla Street and out to Cayuga Lake itself. Many of the boat houses were small, with living quarters above the storage areas. The business passed on to members of his family, and it was operated for a number of years by his daughter, Ruth Pierce and her son Robert. In 1967 Clarence Cleveland bought a partial share, and a few years later he took total control. In the early 1980's he sold it to his three sons Dan, Tom, and Jeff who, as this book is written, operate three boathouses with 120 slips on the 11-acre plot of land. The exact date of this postcard view is not known, but the styles of the boats would suggest the first or second decades of the century. Fortunately someone has written in the margin of the card the name of the establishment, as otherwise we wouldn't know. Notice that the artist-imposed American Flags are flying in a stiff breeze, while the water is at almost a dead calm.

Stewart Park was first known as Renwick Park, after the Renwick family which owned the land from 1790 to the mid-1890's. Edwin C. Stewart, the Mayor when the city purchased the property in 1921, died before his term was completed and left $150,000 in his will for park development. In 1914 the Wharton brothers established a silent movie studio here; between then and 1919 such stars as Francis X. Bushman, Beverly Bayne, Norma Talmadge, Lionel Barrymore, and Pearl White starred in Ithaca-made films . . . including "The Mysteries of

Myra", "The Exploits of Elaine", "The Secret of the Storm County", "The Adopted Son" and, during World War I, "The Eagle's Eye" (starring King Baggot and Marguerite Snow), "In The Air" (featuring Lieutenant Bert Hall), and "Patria". Probably some scenes in "The Perils of Pauline" also were made in Ithaca. The park and its buildings were first developed by the Cayuga Lake Electric Railway, in 1894, an offshoot of the Ithaca Street Railway, as a means of increasing patronage of its lines—a common practice at the turn-of-the-century. Note the trolley car coming 'round the bend.

Cayuga Lake and Renwick Park, Ithaca, N. Y.

Just to the left of this picture was the Remington Salt Works, in which the owners apparently took great pride. They issued invitations in the form of mailing pieces sent throughout the region inviting visitors to visit the salt works, presumably to try to convince them that 'Crystaline Table Salt'—the plant's premier product—would be considered worthy of their use once they witnessed how it was produced. To the right a few hundred yards is the first piece of land that juts into the lake, seen as one travels northward along Cayuga's east shore, McKinney's Point. For many years at the southern edge of this point was a piece of real estate that always caused this writer's father to laugh when he drove by. On the shingled roof of a garage belonging to one of the lake cottages were carefully-laid shingles of a contrasting color spelling out the word 'MONEYSUNK'; the feature remains today, although on the side of the cottage. In the distance is the boat dock jutting out from Renwick Park, and the buildings behind it were probably in full use by the Wharton Movie Studios at the time this picture was published as the automobile is of that vintage.

36

Ithaca, N.Y. Pier at Renwick.

The *Frontenac*, a classic side-wheel steamboat, made its maiden voyage on June 4, 1870. 135 feet long with a 22 foot beam and complete with rocking-beam, it was operated by the Cayuga Lake Transportation Company and provided a convenient means of northward travel for up to 350 passengers from Ithaca in connection with the railroads. A morning connection with the train operating between Sayre and Geneva took passengers on board in time for breakfast on a 3 ½ hour cruise to Cayuga, 40 or so miles to the north, with intermediate stops at various resorts—in time to meet the New York Central trains. The *Frontenac* was destroyed by fire on July 27, 1907, with the loss of seven lives. Its wreckage was hauled to the surface during World War II during a scrap drive.

Central New York State is blessed with enormous quantities of salt beneath its surface, and over the years Cayuga Lake has had associated with it a variety of mines and plants to extract this common but valuable commodity. The Cayuga Lake Salt Works at Ludlowville, eight miles north of Ithaca on the lake's east shore, is here seen in its glory days when the Auburn Branch of the Lehigh Valley Railroad could count on plenty of revenue each year from the carloads of sodium chloride that it hauled to distant markets. The salt works was started in 1892 by three men from Warsaw, New York; eventually after various financial difficulties it became part of the International Salt Company. Salt that is mined from deep beneath the waters of Cayuga Lake is very much in the public eye throughout the northeastern part of the United States, as a large proportion of what is taken is used to melt snow and ice from roads and highways. The trade-off to this safety measure is reduced service life of our automobiles and trucks, so it's a mixed blessing.

Renwick Pier, at the head of Cayuga Lake, was a busy place around the turn-of-the-century when steamboat activity was at its peak. The *Iroquois* and the *Mohawk* joined the mighty *Frontenac* on Cayuga in 1901, serving the Brown Transportation Line.

If there's an over-abundance of views of Cayuga Lake steamers in this book, there's a good reason for it. There's just nothing that can better capture the spirit of a time when life was a little bit slower-paced. Not that everything was rosy in those days, but it is sometimes fun to reflect on how nice it must have been when life wasn't as hectic as it seems today. A pleasant lake cruise surely creates the mood of those turn-of-the-century times, and the intent of this book is to put readers in the mood of the past — for better or worse.

Frontenac Beach, Cayuga La

The pretty Frontenac is awaiting passengers as Frontenac Beach, now the location of Camp Barton which belongs to the Baden Powell Council of the Boy Scouts of America, located 13 miles north of Ithaca on the west shore of Lake Cayuga. Generations of Boy Scouts will recall, perhaps with a bit of nostalgia, the camp song penned in 1934 to the tune of the lilting college football march "Washington and Lee Swing":

"We have a Boy Scout Camp at Frontenac —
a camp that's really worth your while;
we've seen a dozen other Boy Scout camps,
but ours has got them skinned a mile (or two or three).
You'd better come to Frontenac today,
put on your shorts and come prepared to stay.
When camping time rolls 'round again you'll say—again you'll say
Camp Barton is the place for me!"

of Steamer Frontenac Cayuga Lake, Burned July 27, 1907.

Completely aside from the tragic loss of life, this scene of the tangled wreckage of the *Frontenac* is enough to make a grown man cry. Note the men working their way around the remains of the once-glorious vessel, and the forlorn-looking rocking beam that turned the crankshaft on its final revolution on July 27, 1907. The message written on the edge of the card refers to a special train on the Lehigh Valley, no doubt having had some association with this nautical disaster.

39

Cayuga Lake, N.Y., Steamer Mohawk, Brown Line.

These two pictures present something of a mystery. Are they the same boat, with different names, or were two practically-identical boats operated on Cayuga Lake? Clearly the vessel *Iroquois* in the top picture on page 38 is different from both, although the *Mohawk* in that picture is the same as the boat above. Lifeboat accomodations appear to be rather skimpy should the considerable crowd on the *Mohawk* be forced to abandon ship for any reason. Today a scene like the one below would give EPA officials fits, with great clouds of black smoke from the burning of soft coal smothering the lake and its frontage properties. But in the days when such craft were common on Cayuga Lake, such belching stacks—whether on boats or connected to factories—were considered a sure sign of prosperity and good times. Names from central New York's Indian tribes, together with those from Greek and Roman regions, abound in our area as titles for things and places. Ithaca itself is of Greek origin. Marcellus, Hector, Ulysses, Etna, Ovid, Varna, Syracuse, and Homer are but a few classical examples; the list is a long one.

Steamer "Iroquois," Cayuga Lake, N.Y.

Boating on Cayuga Lake, Ithaca, N.Y.

Dear Father:
Here's to ten more voyages
safely made.
Yours
S. H. Worden

There's hardly anything more inviting than a pleasant outing on Cayuga Lake during the summer season, whether it be sailing, canoeing, yachting, or speedboating. This early card, printed in "Frankfort o/Main," Germany, certainly is beguiling, but looks can be deceiving. Cayuga Lake can be very treacherous, and it has claimed the lives of many unwary boaters. With depths ranging from four to six hundred feet, it is always cold, and its slender long configuration between hills is such that hazardous winds and waves often arise suddenly to trap those who would be careless about such matters. For many years, Cornell University authorities posted signs in prominent places all over the campus cautioning students to be careful when venturing on the seemingly placid waters. The tiny cockpits in this wooden craft from pre-fiberglass days suggest that it was built strictly for sport, with comfort a minor consideration.

One of the greatest rowing coaches anywhere was Charles Courtney who was on the Cornell staff from 1885 to 1920. The result of this stern taskmaster's work was that Cornell had some of the greatest crews of all time during that era, generating much favorable publicity for the university. Crew races were of interest to the betting crowd much as football and basketball are today — legally or otherwise! Cayuga Lake inlet was the primary area for rowing activity, and the class of 1890 gave this boat house so familiar to Ithacans. Romeyn

Berry, writing for the Cornell Alumni News, tells how Mr. Courtney was so anxious to get his crews into practice in the spring that he would dynamite the ice on the inlet with explosives surreptitiously purchased under "miscellaneous expenses" of the Athletic Association. So popular was the sport that the highly illegal dynamiting within city limits was conveniently unnoticed by Ithaca officials.

The Lehigh Valley's Auburn branch observation train was generally a pretty lengthy affair, so when it was being made up it was necessary to separate the cars so as not to block street crossings. This happy throng is eagerly anticipating the short journey up and back down the east side of Cayuga Lake, with partisans of various colleges aboard the makeshift seating in gondola number 29 765 anxious to cheer their favorite crew on to victory. The Auburn branch of the Lehigh was abandoned north of Ludlowville as far as Aurora in the early 1950's, but when the New York State Electric and Gas Corporation planned Millikan Station to open in 1955 at Lake Ridge, 14 miles north of Ithaca, the railroad relaid 6 ½ miles of track to bring coal for conversion into electricity by this big steam power plant. In the 1980's, close to a million tons of coal yearly pass over these tracks, in 80-car unit trains that are loaded at Clarksburg, Pennsylvania. They are routed via the Baltimore and Ohio Railroad to Salamanca, New York, where they are switched to tracks of Conrail which owns the remains of the Erie Railroad and the Lehigh. The trains carry about 7000 tons of coal, averaging 2 to 3 trains per week.

Another view of the Lehigh observation train, as passengers take their seats soon to witness the grand sporting event of the day. Has anyone ever discovered a better way to witness a crew race than the Lehigh's observation train? 1936 was the last year the train ran, and no race was watched, because the event was called off at 8 p.m. The winds failed to die down and darkness took over thus making it quite impossible for events to proceed. The fine brick station of the Delaware Lackawanna and Western's Owego branch is just to the left of the picture. Billboards posted on the buildings along Fulton Street promote Tip Top Bread, a brand of beer whose maker cannot be distinguished, and Weber and Fields—a famed vaudeville team of the day—playing "Hokey Pokey." The DL & W Railroad has been gone since the 1950's, and the terminal now serves as a bus station.

For years, a big part of "Spring Day" at Cornell was the traditional crew race between the Ivy League colleges, on a course close to the east shore of Cayuga Lake, and the Lehigh Valley Railroad capitalized on public interest in the event by running on its Ithaca-Auburn branch a special train of gondola cars fitted with bleachers to seat hundreds of spectators. By this means it was possible to follow the entire length of the race, as we see here looking north toward McKinney's Point. The umbrella at the lower right suggests the possibility of rain; note the conductor at the lower left of this card which was postmarked in 1907. This train was operated as early as 1899. A locomotive with a Wooten firebox capable of burning hard coal was often used, to minimize the smoke nuisance.

Following the Race, Observation Train, Ithaca, N. Y.

The culmination of Spring Day was the late-afternoon crew race between Ivy League teams, after the winds had died down so that the waters were sufficiently placid so that they would not swamp the shallow draft shells. This is obviously the finish line, as is apparent from the cluster of boats on the near side of the course, and this is a view passengers on the Lehigh Valley observation train would have seen. Note the long and powerful speedboat (perhaps carrying referees and officials) in front of the group of boats, and the many expensive yachts on the far side of the course. An artist has added interest to the picture with a "faked-in" single-engined biplane, which presumably would have been flying out of Ithaca's airport which was just to the left of this scene.

Finish of a Varsity Boat Race, Cayuga Lake.
Ithaca, N. Y.

The Lehigh Valley Railroad's showcase train was the Black Diamond Express, which covered the route from New York City to Buffalo via Ithaca, with connections to Philadelphia. Its inaugural run was on 18 May, 1896; its final trip was on 11 May, 1959 and in the intervening 63 years it provided the finest in service for Cornellians and Ithacans. Robert Archer in his monumental history of the Lehigh notes "the road touted it as 'The Handsomest Train in the World'. The lead car was a combination baggage and cafe car outfitted with a

Black Diamond Express between New York, Philadelphia, and Buffalo, Lehigh Valley, R.R

library and smoking room for gentlemen . . . Kitchen and dining facilities were to the rear of the car, presided over by chefs whose culinary artistry in 'preparing and serving substantials and delicacies in most appetizing fashion' was glowingly extolled by a zealous passenger department . . . the second and third cars were day coaches equipped with smoking rooms and finished with interiors of polished Mexican mahogany, accentuated by inlaid bevelled French plate mirrors. . . Bringing up the rear were parlor cars 'Lehigh', 'Ganoga', and 'Seneca', complete with open observation platforms and suffocating velvet interior decor so favored in the late Victorian period." The artist-contrived out-of-perspective British-made postcard dates from around 1905.

MOTOR CAR, THE LATEST THING IN RAILROAD EQUIPMENT

ОW IN USE ON THE "SHORT LINE" BETWEEN AUBURN AND ITHACA, N

Ithaca was tied to the rest of New York's early-20th-Century network of interurban railways by a trolley line towards Auburn, which ascended the hill starting near Renwick Park on a roadbed which even today is apparent in many places. At one time two McKeen "Windsplitter" gasoline-engine cars (as depicted here) were used on this route, but they were badly underpowered for this service and could only make the grade if they had a substantial "head start" by gathering a great deal of momentum on the flats. The car was designed by William McKeen, Superintendent of Motive Power for the Union Pacific Railroad, and it used a 5-inch Morse silent chain drive (an Ithaca product) from the engine to the single drive axle. About 150 such cars were built.

Ithaca's passenger terminal on the Lehigh Valley Railroad was one of that road's busiest, from the standpoint of passenger traffic —thanks to the large number of Cornell students who traveled to and from New York City. It was opened in 1898, and was built to designs of architect A. G. Wood. An admirable service provided for many years by the railroad was having a Pullman sleeping car at the station, available for boarding after 9 p.m. New York-bound travelers could go to bed anytime after that hour and awake in New York City, just in time for breakfast, thanks to having been switched to the east-bound train in the middle of the night. Somehow today's travel, with all of its high technology, doesn't seem quite as luxurious!

These proud railway men surely are pleased to be photographed with their high-stepping iron steed #1676. The Lehigh Valley Railroad at one time owned about 1,000 locomotives, and there were about 100 of these class J-55 ½ six-wheelers. 1676 was built by the American Locomotive Works in 1907, rebuilt by Baldwin in November of 1923, and eventually scrapped in February of 1934. She was designed to work on 205 psi steam pressure, featured 69 inch diameter drivers, and weighed around 207,000 pounds. Locomotives of this type,

with the engineer's cab located midway along the length of the boiler, were commonly referred to as "Hubbards", because of the presumed resemblance of his limited quarters to "Mother Hubbard's cupboard." Wooten fireboxes were designed to burn anthracite (hard coal) which has less heat output per pound than does soft coal, thus necessitating a larger grate area. This in turn left little room behind the boiler for the engineer's station, which accounts for it being in the central location.

When this card was postmarked in 1913, Ithaca's Delaware, Lackawanna and Western station of the Ithaca-Owego Branch was just a year old. The DL and W enjoyed the reputation of being, mile for mile, the most highly developed railroad in America, and this lovely and substantial brick structure suggests just that. It's still very functional, albeit as a bus terminal. The Ithaca and Owego was the second railroad chartered in New York State, in 1828, and it carried its first passengers the full 34 miles to Ithaca from Owego in 1834. It was originally drawn by horses, and the descent down South Hill was made by inclined planes from approximately where the Borg-Warner plant is today. 1840 saw the first steam locomotive; 1850 saw the planes abandoned in favor of new trackage which was built with a double switchback to handle the gradient. The DL & W acquired the line in the 1850's; the last train to Ithaca ran on December 4, 1956. A sleeper from New York ran as late as 1933, and from the mid 'thirties special holiday trains were run to accommodate Cornell students returning to or coming from the "Big Apple". The DL & W's time to the city was less than that of the Lehigh Valley, thus providing an incentive for travelers to make use of this fine facility instead of the Lehigh's station, just a few hundred feet away on the other side of the Cayuga Lake Inlet.

A postcard view of the Ithaca Lackawanna Station in its hey-day with rolling stock nearby proved impossible to find for inclusion in this book. The next-best thing, in order to indicate the type of equipment typically seen on the railroad running between Ithaca and Owego, is this station just 12 miles down the track in Caroline. In a day when automobiles are universal, it's interesting to reflect on the fact that not many generations ago small communities everywhere were dependent on the local railroad for citizens to travel farther than their team of horses could conveniently take them. The presence of an express wagon suggests that the agent who held forth at the Caroline depot handled a good many packages for the locals. It was a time when rural folk relied on shipments from mail-order firms like Sears and Roebuck and Montgomery Ward for everything from pocket watches to sheep-shears to entire pre-cut homes, and most of these goods came on the tracks either directly through the railway company's agent or via the railway mails. This card was postmarked in 1920.

LEHIGH VALLEY VIADUCT, BROOKTON, N. Y.

Ezra Cornell invested an estimated 2 million dollars in the Ithaca and Cortland Railroad; this became part of the Elmira, Cortland and Northern Railroad, which around 1905 became the EC & N division of the Lehigh Valley Railroad. Local wags referred to this as the "Empty, Crooked, and Nasty." It extended at one time from Elmira to Camden, New York, passing through "East Ithaca" along the way. Near what we now call Brooktondale, whose station was exactly six miles down the track east of Ithaca, the road passed over this spindly 800-foot long, 85-foot high steel viaduct, was constructed in 1894 to replace one of wood built in 1875. The viaduct in the picture was damaged in the great 1935 flood, and service between Elmira and East Ithaca never resumed.

...IGH VALLEY DEPOT
...ST ITHACA, N. Y.

Sad and forlorn was the East Ithaca station of the EC & N Division of the Lehigh Valley Railroad after it fell into disuse in the 1940's, even though the railroad continued to bring coal to the Cornell heating plant for a number of years afterwards. Fortunately for the cause of historic preservation, the structure has been saved and now serves as a restaurant and watering hole on the Judd Falls Road, just a few hundred feet east of this location on Maple Avenue. The scene looks to the south toward Besemers, Brooktondale and Willseyville; trains headed to Elmira were discontinued in that direction in 1935. Thrilled indeed were the youngsters (your writer amongst them) who on occasion were permitted by the trainmen to give the big steam engine a 180 on the hand-operated turntable. In the late 1930's one train a day (usually the engine and one old coach) arrived around 2 p.m. from Canastota. It was necessary to turn the engine for the return trip, which left around 5:30 p.m. The restaurant is Ithaca's sole remaining reminder of Ezra Cornell's enormous investment and his dreams for rail service direct to the university.

Ithaca had two steel truss rail bridges parallel to Cayuga Street, crossing Fall Creek — one for the trolleys, and one for the Auburn-Ithaca branch of the Lehigh Valley Railroad. Evidence suggests that this is the Lehigh Bridge, for it's a Whipple trapezoidal truss of a type favored by John W. Murphy, chief engineer of that road for a number of years, and it seems heavier than what the street cars would have needed. Further, no catenary of wires to supply energy to street cars is apparent. Squire Whipple was one of the first engineers

Copyright 1908 by the Corner Book Stores.
Along Fall Creek, Ithaca, N. Y.

in America who was able to design bridges by an analytical and mathematical approach. Lehigh records indicate that this bridge, if indeed it was theirs, was number A308C: A designates the Auburn-Ithaca branch, 308 means that it was between mileposts 308 and 309, and C means that it was the third bridge within that mile. Files in the possession of railroad historian Herb Trice indicate that the truss was 125 feet long, measured from centers of the end pins — it's a true pin-connected truss — and that it was built in 1883. Sometime after 1902 it was replaced by a plate-girder bridge.

This throng, gathered at one of Ithaca's rail stations, is waiting to greet the Cornell football team on its return from a victory over Harvard, 10 to 0, October 24, 1915. That was the year that Cornell had its first national championship team, with nine wins and no losses. Scenic commercial post cards, printed in large numbers, give a marvelous general view of a community's development over the years. Photo post cards such as this one, produced by a local photographer for sale on a limited basis, offer a micro-history by showing special events and moods of the era in which they were made. For example, it is clear that this was a chilly day. It's also clear that it was a time when men's haberdashery businesses prospered — you'll look hard to find a man in the picture without either a necktie or a hat!

Early in Cornell's existence, it became apparent that many would-be university students were arriving in Ithaca ill-prepared for the rigors of college-level work. In 1868 Professor Lucian Wait of the department of mathematics decided to do something about this, so he initiated, with the approval of President Andrew D. White, a preparatory school located in Cascadilla Hall. Between its founding and the turn-of-the-century it carried on in a building on what became Wait Avenue, west of the Cornell campus, as well as in the structure

Copyright 1905 by the Rotograph Co·
A 5209   Cascadilla School, Ithaca, N. Y.

seen here located at Oak and Summit Avenues, where it continues to this day. In 1890 it was incorporated as The Cascadilla College Preparatory School. During the early years it was a regular residence school with dormitories. In 1925 it became exclusively a day school and operated as such for a number of years, but in the 1980's two dormitories are operated. One of them, for women, is the former piano salesroom and home of Richard Flight on Dryden Road, in front of which remains a fiberglass grand piano that has become a local landmark.

Copyright 1905 by the Rotograph Co·
A 5185   Cascadilla recreation Building, Ithaca, N. Y.

Did you ever see this? When are you coming to see me? I will write a long letter to on soon. Bess.

In its earlier days when the Cascadilla School was a resident institution, this structure at the head of Cayuga Lake and adjacent to Renwick Park provided a fine place for recreation, athletics, and boating. It dates from the turn-of-the-century, apparently roughly coincident with the time that the Ithaca Street Railway company built up Renwick Park as an amusement attraction, and the convenient trolley cars made it an easy matter for Cascadilla students to get back and forth from their classroom activities on East Hill. In the 1930's the Cascadilla School fell on financial hard times, and the City of Ithaca took over this building.

Few would argue the point that the setting of Ezra Cornell's university is one of the most beautiful in the United States, if not the world, and over the years much has been done to link the natural scenery of the immediate area with the campus design. A related area is Cascadilla gorge on the south side of the campus. For many years these sylvan walkways named in honor of Professor Goldwin Smith on both embankments of Cascadilla Creek just south of Hoy Field have provided not only a restful and relaxing place for walks by harried stu-

dents, staff, and administrators, but have been a wonderful place for the youngsters of Ithaca's East Hill to ride their bicycles, safe from the dangers of the frequently-busy streets.

Sheldon Court, Ithaca, N. Y.

Generations of Cornell students recall that their books and supplies were purchased primarily from two stores, the Cornell Campus Store, for years located in the basement of Barnes Hall, and the Triangle Book Store located in Sheldon Court, a substantial private dormitory in Collegetown. When the building was willed by a member of the Sheldon family in the late 1940's to Father Divine, a well-known Black cult leader, Evan J. Morris (owner of the book store) was able to buy the entire property. There is no indication that Father Divine intended to establish one of his "Heavens" on College Avenue even if Mr. Morris had not bought the place, although the thought probably passed a few minds.

Cascadilla Hall was built in the mid-1860's, near where Otis Eddy's cotton factory had been located, at the north end of what we know as Eddy Street. It was intended to be a water-cure hospital, following one of the favored medical treatments of the day, but this scheme was short-lived and the newly-established Cornell University was able to purchase it at a low price for use as an office building and a residence for both faculty and students. It has served a variety of uses over the years. Note the trolley tracks at the right.

William H. Sage paid for the beautiful stone arch bridge that forms the entrance to Cornell's campus from College Avenue, first named Heustis Street. While Ithaca and Cornell are blessed with the scenic beauty of the gorges that penetrate the hillsides, they are cursed with their tragic side, too. The bridges provide a convenient place from which individuals may leap to escape life's realities, and the number who will seek this way out is fairly predictable from year to year. One such person, known to only a few Cornellians, was the Englishman George Bennett who had been Willard Straight's valet and who admired the man greatly. George (a friend of this writer) ended his life in the late 1940's by stepping from the side of this bridge. He had never recovered from the emotional shock of the death of his beloved Major Straight who succumbed to pneumonia in France in 1919.

Kappa Alpha fraternity, the structure under the flagpole, was destroyed to provide space for the complex of engineering buildings now located in that immediate area. The fraternity was built on land leased by the university. Designed by William H. Miller, it was constructed at a cost of $16,000, and opened in 1883. This move to let a private organization use campus space was controversial, but President Andrew D. White was highly in favor of such "private dormitories" and his views prevailed, at least in a few instances. Kappa Alpha was

ENTRANCE TO THE CAMPUS IN WINTER.   CORNELL UNIVERSITY.

founded in 1825 at Union College; the local chapter dates from 1868, the same year that Cornell began. The finial atop Sage College can be seen poking itself above the horizon formed by the treetops just to the right of the flag; alas, this delightful architectural feature capping the Victorian splendor of the building had to be removed in the 1950's. The rather gloomy winter sky presents an interesting contrast to the snow-laden trees that surround Cascadilla Gorge.

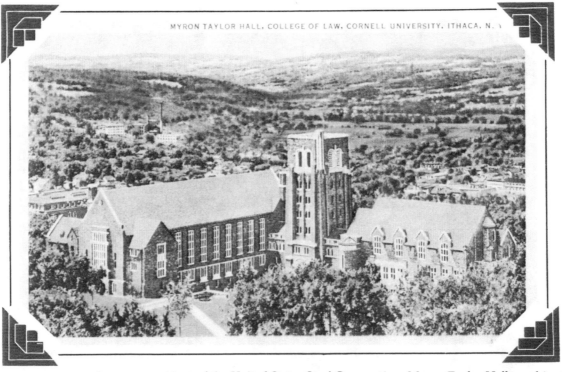

MYRON TAYLOR HALL, COLLEGE OF LAW, CORNELL UNIVERSITY, ITHACA, N. Y

Myron C. Taylor ('94) rose to become president of the United States Steel Corporation. Myron Taylor Hall was his gift to the university as a home for the law school, and it opened in 1930. In his latter years Mr. Taylor served as President Franklin D. Roosevelt's personal envoy to The Vatican.

The beautiful law library within Myron Taylor Hall probably features more cubic feet per occupant than any other space at Cornell, and the picture makes it clear that the structure was erected with a minimum of budgetary constraint. It, together with Anabel Taylor Hall which opened in 1952 to house the Cornell United Religious Work, was one of the last Gothic-style edifices to be built on the university's campus; the latter was a gift in memory of Myron Taylor's wife. The third and last magnificent structure in the Gothic tradition is Teagle Hall (not pictured), the men's gymnasium, opened in 1954, the gift of Mr. and Mrs. Walter C. Teagle, ('00).

Anabel Taylor Hall, Cornell University, Ithaca, N. Y.

In Cornell's early years a number of faculty members built homes on the campus. One still remains, that of the first President, Andrew D. White; it served for a number of years as an art museum. One of the last private homes to be demolished was Sage Cottage, located where the Gannett Medical Clinic now sits. It was originally the home of Professor Albert N. Prentiss who was a Professor of Botany and Horticulture and who doubled as Superintendent of Buildings and Grounds and tripled for a time as Director of Manual Labor. For a time

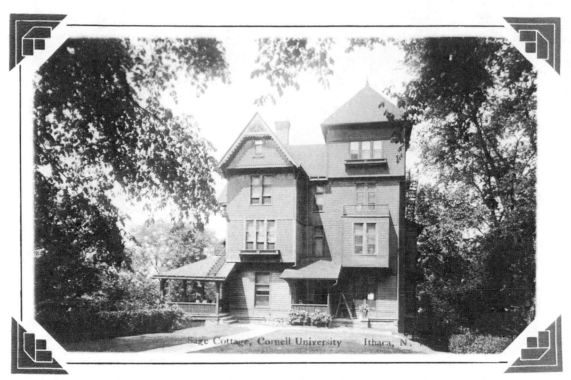

Sage Cottage, Cornell University   Ithaca, N.

the university had an unsuccessful program of manual works by which Ezra Cornell hoped that many students could earn their tuition monies while in school. Sage Cottage served for housing women for a number of years. In 1914 it became the "University Club", a resting place for weary professors and a dining spot which, according to Morris Bishop, was "much made over, always for the worse."

OLIN HALL OF CHEMICAL ENGINEERING, CORNELL UNIVERSITY, ITHACA, N. Y.

Economic constraints and changes in technology of construction make it impracticable for an institution such as Cornell to have each new building look exactly like the others. In 1942, when Olin Hall of Chemical Engineering was dedicated there was considerable public controversy as to its appearance, but the architects — Shreve, Lamb, and Harmon (the same firm which designed the Empire State Building in New York City) did what most sensible building designers do when they don't have an unlimited budget. They took the best

elements from the surrounding buildings —the brick and native stone—and combined them in a manner to create what today most observers would agree is a most attractive and affordable concept. Olin Hall was the first building of the "new" engineering campus on the south edge of Cornell's land. It was the gift of Franklin W. Olin '86, who gave $685,000 to construct it as a memorial to his son, Franklin W. Olin Jr, ('12). The elder Olin was a baseball star when he was a student, and he played professional ball during summers while in attendance at Cornell—a practice not considered proper in this day of highly-organized professional sports and collegiate athletic associations.

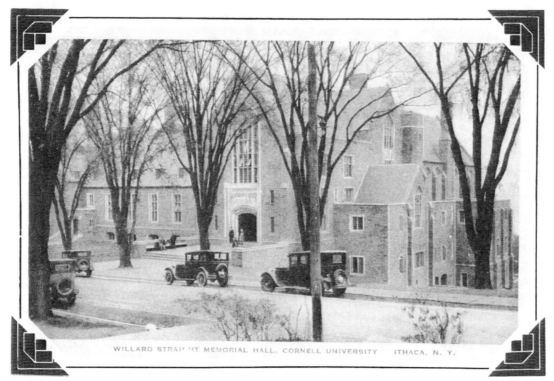

WILLARD STRAIGHT MEMORIAL HALL, CORNELL UNIVERSITY   ITHACA, N. Y.

Willard Dickerman Straight graduated from Cornell's school of architecture in 1901, and then went on to spend part of his altogether too short life as a member of the Diplomatic Corps and another as a partner in one of the Morgan banking groups. He married Dorothy Payne Whitney who, upon Straight's death shortly after the close of World War I, used a considerable part of her inherited fortune to present Cornell with this magnificent structure to his memory. An outstanding feature of its interior is the "Memorial Room" designed in the style of a great hall in a British manor house. In Mr. Straight's will he requested that his own estate be used to make Cornell a more livable place for students, (or words to that effect). The building went into service in 1925, and judging by the styles of the automobiles shown, this picture was made shortly thereafter.

Franchot Tone '27, who went on to gain fame and fortune in Hollywood, was the star in the play — *The Contrasts* — by Royal Tyler on the occasion of the opening of Willard Straight's Little Theatre. The beautiful artwork on the walls was the work of muralist James Monroe Hewlett, who was born in Lawrence, New York in 1868, and who died there in 1941 after a distinguished career. He studied art at Columbia University; did murals in many banks and public buildings, and was a full member of the National Academy [NY 1931]. Pro-

THE THEATER, Willard Straight Hall, Cornell, Ithaca, N. Y.

fessor Walter Stainton of the Department of Speech and Drama was in charge of the facility in the 1930's and 40's, and he enjoyed bringing early silent films to the theatre. He engaged a gifted pianist and student named Ruth Simon to re-create the atmosphere of the early days of the "nickelodeon" by providing a musical accompaniment to whatever scenes were taking place on the silver screen. Your writer had the privilege of being her relief pianist, and in so doing, gained a lasting love of this almost-forgotten musical art form.

When Sage Avenue ran kitty-corner on a line from where Myron Taylor Hall now is to the front of what was then known as Sage College, it offered a most pleasing panorama of that area of Cornell's campus. Carpenter Hall, which houses administrative offices and the library of the engineering college, now straddles that road-bed, and the southeast corner of Olin Hall just broaches it. Note the "x" that someone put on this postcard, noting the finial which was removed in the 1950's. Old grads who attended Cornell when the campus had many more acres of grass than it does today and plenty of woodsy areas to boot, are often aghast at how buildings have usurped the spots they recall with such affection. Various administrations over the years have tried valiantly to preserve as much as possible of the beauty of the thousand or so acres that comprise the campus proper, consistent with their mandates to develop the physical plant to meet the constantly increasing demands placed on a great university.

Construction of Sage College was started in 1872, designed by Professor Babcock as an educational and residence structure for women, complete with a dining hall and gymnasium. Full occupancy was not achieved until several years after its completion; not every woman enrolled at Cornell was enthusiastic about residing there, nor were they all able to afford it. Its construction and design was marked by much tugging and hauling between Ezra Cornell, the architect, and President Andrew D. White as to design, costs and Babcock's fees, over and above his salary as a Professor. Kermit Parsons suggests that it was probably the largest building constructed in Ithaca to that time.

Sage Chapel is one of only two buildings to merit an entire chapter in Parsons' book, the other being the library. The original building was financed by Henry Sage; its architect was Charles Babcock, both professor of architecture and an Episcopal clergyman. Since its dedication in 1875, a number of changes and additions have been made, the last major one being an extension towards Willard Straight in 1940 at which time a new pipe organ was installed in the back of the sanctuary. In spite of all these alterations, the architectural integrity of the structure has been preserved; a true bulwark against modernity. Within the building lie the remains of Ezra Cornell and his wife, their eldest son Alonzo, Andrew D. White and his wife, John McGraw, Jennie McGraw and Willard Fiske, and Edmund Ezra Day.

When the newly-founded university declared itself as 'Unsectarian', which Cornell did back in the 1860's, it was denounced by many clerics as nothing short of ungodly, heretical, blasphemous, and other terms that suggested that no God-fearing parent should permit their offspring to attend such a place. It was a time when churches controlled many of the colleges and universities across the land. Ezra Cornell was born a Quaker, but he married Mary Ann Wood, an Episcopalian, whereupon he was "read out of meeting." The Quakers offered to reinstate him, should he recognize the error of his ways, but young Ezra could not regard his marriage as a mistake; for the rest of his life he remained independent in his religious thinking, although he frequently met with the Unitarians. He saw to it that no one ecclesiastical group was ever dominant on the campus, and while it was important to him and other early leaders that Cornell students have available on-campus religious services, Sage Chapel has never had a permanent cleric in charge. Services have always been offered by visiting preachers, priests, and rabbis; thus over the years Cornellians have had the privilege of being exposed to some of the greatest religious thinkers.

Barnes Hall is named for Alfred S. Barnes, the New York publishing tycoon, who gave $40,000 towards construction of a building to be used for religious work. The first such group was the "Cornell University Christian Association", which eventually evolved into C.U.R.W. (Cornell United Religious Work). Over the years the Barnes Hall has housed a wide variety of activities including the Cornell Campus Store. The architect was William Henry Miller, who played such a significant role in the development of campus structures in the formative years of Cornell. Kermit Parsons, the authority on the development of the Cornell Campus, considers Barnes Hall—which was dedicated in 1889 - to be "an architectural gem."

Jennie McGraw Fiske provided handsomely in her will for the development of Cornell's library, a much-needed addition to the expanding university of the 1880's. Unfortunately, Willard Fiske, who she had married shortly before her death, saw fit to contest her will, and the case dragged on for several years before it was actually settled by the United States Supreme Court and the school was in a position to carry out the project. More than one architect was considered for the job, but the commission eventually went to William Henry Miller — a student in Cornell's first class of architects, and one who found favor with Andrew D. White who always showed great interest in a degree of uniformity in the design of Cornell's buildings and their inter-relationships on the campus. Miller's design was considered a great success, and the striking simplicity of his tower has passed the test of time for it has become the symbol of Cornell University and is today recognized all over the world. The building was dedicated on October 7, 1891.

Interior of Library. Cornell University. Ithaca, N. Y. 4/9/07

The main reading room of Cornell's library was 66 by 166 feet, and received excellent natural lighting — to the extent that Ithaca weather permitted—through its 29 windows well above the floor level. Many early Cornell grads will remember their long hours spent within the confines of this space. Note the interesting early lighting equipment, and the bent-wood chairs. Modern fluorescent fixtures added in recent years may have done wonders for the foot-candles at the reading surfaces, but they've surely not helped the quaint Victorian atmosphere.

ROMAN HALL AND THE LIBRARY ON A WINTER'S NIGHT. CORNELL UNIVERSI

Boardman Hall, the university library and its tower, present a most attractive appearance on a snowy night. This photo clearly indicates the common architectural heritage of these two buildings, both designed by William H. Miller — that most prolific architect of major buildings throughout Ithaca and Cornell. One can almost feel the crunch of the snow in this sub-zero scene, devoid of any pedestrian or vehicular activity.

This card is part of "Post Card Series No. 1032, Ithaca, N.Y." by Raphael Tuck & Sons, art publishers to their Majesties the King and Queen. True "deltiologists", as post card collectors are known, vie with each other to collect complete series, from which this is a typical example. Douglass Boardman was a prominent Ithaca lawyer and judge, and the first Dean of the Cornell Law School (established in 1887). William H. Miller, who saw the great new university library rise to his designs, was commissioned to create a new building to meet the needs

of Cornell's future law graduates which would also compliment his other campus structures. Located directly adjacent to the main library, it served from 1890 until it was razed in 1958 to make way for the Olin Research Library. Boardman's home is seen on page 13.

Stimson Hall was erected in 1900-1903 to house Cornell's Medical School, where students could take their first two years of medical training before transferring to New York City. William Henry Miller was the architect, and once again he was able to exercise his considerable talents in maintaining the design integrity and inter-relationship of the stone buildings on the campus as they tied into the original concept of the quadrangle, so dear to the heart of Andrew D. White. Stimson Hall was a donation of Dean Sage, the son of Henry Sage who was such an important early benefactor of the university. It is named for Dr. Lewis A. Stimson, Professor of Surgery and father of Henry L. Stimson, who served as Secretary of State under President Hoover and Secretary of War under Roosevelt during World War II. Note the trolley car tracks, which ran a few more feet to the right side of the picture to a terminus in front of Boardman Hall, and also that the card was distributed by Treman, King & Co., for many years one of Ithaca's leading hardware and industrial supply stores.

Morrill, McGraw, and White Halls face west, away from the Arts Quadrangle, and Central Avenue originally went behind them as we see here. From time to time it has been proposed that a great terrace be built in front of these structures, to enhance the marvelous view across the library slopes to the city and lake in the distance. The westward relocation of Central Avenue was the death knell of that idea. The stone for these buildings, and many other early structures on the campus, was quarried just south of this location, near the intersection of

ALONG CENTRAL AVE., CORNELL UNIVERSITY CAMPUS.
'ACA, NY

Stewart and University Avenues, about where the Bellaire Apartments are located today. In more recent times, stone has been taken from a quarry on the Ellis Hollow Road. Morrill Hall was Cornell's first building, named for Senator Justin Morrill, author of the Land Grant College Act of 1862. This was the act that provided for large sections of Federally-owned western land to be given to states for development of educational institutions; there was avid competition in New York State for its share of this largesse, and only through a great deal of back-stage politicking was Cornell able to acquire the entire amount.

Mc. Graw Hall, Cornell University, Ithaca, N. Y.
Handcolo

Cornell's third building, completed in 1868 to plans of architect Archimedes N. Russell, cost $120,000, and it was given by John McGraw of Dryden. The building is seen here from its rear; its design contemplated it facing west toward a vast terrace which has never been built. The McGraw family fortune was made in lumber, and some of it was used by daughter Jennie to present the new university with its first set of bells, popularly called chimes (to be accurate, a carillon). Their first permanent home was in the tower of McGraw Hall, from where they were eventually moved to the new library tower. Bells added in 1939 make the Cornell "chimes" quite versatile; with 18 bells almost any tune can be, and is, played on them. The "Jennie McGraw Rag" has been performed for years, and your writer recalls being pleasantly startled at hearing, while heading toward an 8-o'clock calculus class in the winter of 1941, the then newly-popular tune "Chattanooga Choo-Choo" as rendered by an obviously gifted and agile carilloneur.

EZRA CORNELL (FOUNDER)
CORNELL UNIVERSITY, ITHACA, N.Y.

ANDREW D. WHITE (FIRST PRESIDENT)

The writer of this card, which was never mailed, inscribed the following on its message space: "These two statues face each other on the Arts College campus. The building in which Andrew D. White is in front of is used for French, English, Economics. In the basement they have a museum with skeletons." (It remains for the reader to wonder if that writer studied English grammar in Goldwin Smith Hall!) Karl Bitter (1867-1915) was the sculptor of the seated Andrew D. White, unveiled in 1915; it was the gift of banker Henry R. Ickelheimer. Ezra Cornell's statue, put on public display in 1918, was sculpted by Herman Atkins MacNeil (1866-1947), an instructor from 1886 to 1889 in the engineering department's short-lived course in Industrial Art.

DAIRY BUILDING

This postcard serves to show that the north wing of Goldwin Smith Hall was indeed once a bastion of agricultural science before it yielded to the pressing requirements for more space for students of Arts and Sciences and became a part of that greater structure which was dedicated in 1906. This building was erected in 1892, and the designers of the rest of Goldwin Smith, architects Carrere and Hastings, were obviously restricted by having to conform to the character of the earlier building by Charles Osborne. The dairy program was obliged to relocate in the vast new expansion of the agricultural campus to the east.

Goldwin Smith, an Oxford-educated professor who came to Cornell at its founding and who taught and lectured off and on for a number of years thereafter, was a revered figure amongst those involved with the humanities. The structure which bears his name was opened in 1906, having been constructed under a common contract with Rockefeller Hall.

The famed museum of casts put on public display in 1894 features replicas of many classical statues from antique Greece and Rome. The collection was assembled by Alfred Emerson, Cornell's first Professor of Archeology and Art. Most are full-sized, and were made from molds formed over the originals. Henry Sage paid for the collection, which was quartered first in McGraw Hall and then went to Goldwin Smith Hall 12 years later. To a student of the classical arts, it's just as important as the collection of kinematic models is to an engineer. The latter is a world-class grouping of devices such as square and oval gears, a myriad of different straight-line drives and special mechanisms of all sorts, all brought from Germany over 100 years ago. All are in display in glassed cabinets in the department of Mechanical Engineering, and both it and the museum of casts exemplify the seriousness of the fledgling university.

View of Cayuga Lake from Cornell University Library.   Ithaca, N. Y.

With scenery like this, is it any wonder that Cornell's campus has been widely hailed as one of the most beautiful in all America? In this rare view the magnificent Jennie McGraw Fiske mansion is very prominent, although when the card was made it already was the Chi Psi fraternity house. Note the woodsy character of what is now the 'library slope', the distant tower in Renwick (Stewart) park at the head of the lake, and the boat piers extending into Cayuga's waters.

Photo. Only, Copyright 1905 by the Rotograph Co.
H 5203   Chi Psi Fraternity Lodge, Ithaca, N. Y.

Jennie McGraw in 1880 used a piece ($300,000) of her inheritance to build a magnificent mansion on a site just below the location of the Johnson Art Museum. She employed William Henry Miller as the architect. While the house was under construction, she travelled in Europe, returning in late 1881 after marrying Willard Fiske, the university's first librarian, in Rome. Within a month she died, and never had the pleasure of occupying this beautiful home. It was purchased by the Chi Psi fraternity in the mid-'nineties for a fraction of its original cost.

64

In December, 1906, the Chi Psi fraternity house—the former Jennie McGraw Fiske mansion— burned to the ground with the tragic loss of seven lives; four students and three Ithaca firemen.

Postcard views abound of fraternity and sorority houses, and one could easily do a whole book of them. This is the only one to appear in this volume; it was deemed appropriate to include it not as a matter of partisan feelings, but to show that the Alpha Psi Chapter—which was founded at Cornell in 1868—was able to have a beautiful new home rise "Phoenix-like" on the site of the ashes of the tragic fire which destroyed their earlier house.

Franklin Hall, College of Electricity,
Cornell University,
Ithaca, N. Y.

Franklin Hall, designed by Professor Charles Babcock, opened in 1882 and housed Cornell's first laboratory for physics, together with laboratories for chemistry. Built of red stone, in contrast to the gray stone of other early Cornell buildings, it has always been controversial as to appearance. In fact, President Jacob Schurman considered it an eyesore, and didn't hesitate to say so. Its roofline has been altered from the one in this view. In 1888 chemistry was moved to Morse Hall, directly adjacent to the west, and in 1889 Professor Robert Thurston, director of Sibley College of Engineering, created America's first department of Electrical Engineering, housed in this building until the 1950's.

Sibley hall for mechanical engineering was constructed in four parts; Hiram Sibley of Rochester, a charter Trustee, gave funds for the first building which today is called West Sibley; it was built in 1870 and extended in 1884. Sibley's fortune was made in the telegraph business. The second part, East Sibley, was given by Hiram W. Sibley (son of Hiram) and completed in 1894. Readers with a penchant for architecture will notice that they "tie right in" with the design of Cornell's first buildings, McGraw, Morrill, and White Halls. The architect

Sibley College, Cornell University, Ithaca, N. Y.

was Archimedes N. Russell. Sibley Dome, the final section, was designed by Arthur N. Gibb ('91), and was also a gift of Hiram W. The Engineering College (except for the Department of Chemical Engineering which had occupied Olin Hall in 1942) moved to the south end of the campus in the 1950's.

Rand Hall, which originally housed machine shops and electrical laboratories for the College of Engineering resembles more a factory than a university building. It was the gift of Florence Rand Lang in 1912 as a family memorial, and most particularly in memory of her brother, Jasper Rand ('97). In recent years the building has housed a computer center and drafting rooms for the school of architecture, among other uses. Note the trolley tracks on the far side of East Avenue.

Kermit Parsons in his book *The Cornell Campus* tells the interesting tale of how Lincoln Hall, which became the first building especially erected for Civil Engineering and Architecture, was designed to be of brick. Andrew D. White was furious on discovering this, and he exhorted the Trustees to stick with stone, to match the other buildings on the "Arts Quadrangle." The Trustees acquiesed and appropriated an additional $7,000 to build it of stone, but this was not enough to do the entire building — thus the back ended up in brick, much to the displeasure of President Charles K. Adams. The structure was erected in 1888-89, to designs of Charles Babcock, Cornell's first Professor of Architecture. These were difficult economic times for the new university, and such expenditures could not be taken lightly.

Lincoln Hall, Cornell University, Ithaca, N. Y.

This interesting photocard features a group of Cornell civil engineering students, class of 1910. The card is postmarked June of 1907, so one may reasonably surmise that these are sophomores in a design laboratory in Lincoln Hall. The photographer was able to capture their undivided attention, and chances are they were happy for a bit of relief from the tedium of calculating the stresses in the chords and tension members of a Pratt or Howe truss to support railroad track spanning a mythical chasm. In this era railroad engineering was an important part of the training of all civil engineers, and the theories and mathematics of bridge design in particular took up a good share of every undergraduate's time.

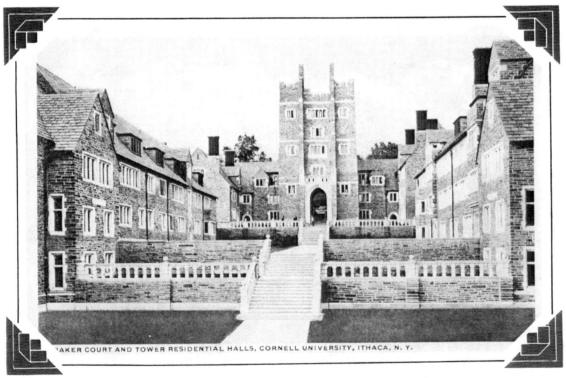

BAKER COURT AND TOWER RESIDENTIAL HALLS, CORNELL UNIVERSITY, ITHACA, N. Y.

George F. Baker, the same New York banker who gave the funds for the Baker Laboratory of Chemistry, gave the university $300,000 to construct this group of dormitories around a courtyard, opened in 1916. The architects developed the structure in such a way that additional sections could be added from time to time and still maintain the over-all design integrity. George C. Boldt, a wealthy hotelman and trustee, funded a further part of this dormitory complex, and alumni funds were spent for still another section. Visitors to New York's Thousand Islands will recognize the name Boldt from the famous 'castle' on Heart Island in the St. Lawrence River.

Cornell's Baker Laboratory of Chemistry was built soon after World War I, to designs of architects Arthur N. Gibb '90 and Frank M. Day. The cornerstone-laying took place on October 21, 1921, with University President Livingston Farrand presiding first over ceremonies at Bailey Hall, where several speeches were endured, and then continuing with a procession (with Professor Charles L. Durham as Faculty Marshal) to the site. There Mr. Gibb handed a box of records to Harold A. Ley, the contractor, who placed the box within the cornerstone. Mr. George F. Baker, the banker who had given $1,500,000 for the building, laid the cornerstone. Perhaps wearied by the ceremonies, Baker's remarks were brief. He said "I am glad that my offering is welcome, and I hope it will be useful."

Local rumor has always had it that when John D. Rockefeller saw, or learned, how the $250,000 he had donated for the construction of a building for the physics department had been spent, he was so displeased that he never made another donation to the university. Whether this is true or not, and whether the rather plain building with its unfinished look (especially on the interior) resulted from having tried to spread the money thin in order to obtain maximum floor area, or if some of the money was spent on equipment instead of construction, remains a matter of conjecture. Goldwin Smith Hall and Rockefeller Hall were built under one contract, and they went into service around 1906.

John T. Parson ('91), a Professor of Civil Engineering and a devotee of the sport of ice hockey, built and maintained a rink on Beebe Lake, starting in 1896. Many Cornellians have fond memories of the Johnny Parson Club, a winter sports house that opened in 1923 on the west end of the lake, that housed not only a faculty club and 200-seat restaurant, but a "warming room" where generations of Ithacans and Cornellians put on and removed their ice skates, and took refuge from time to time during their skating sessions to gain a bit of warm relief from the frigid temperatures of the Ithaca winters.

SKATING ON BEEBEE LAKE, CORNELL UNIVERSITY, ITHACA, N.Y.

A favorite cooling-off spot for Ithaca's younger set was the deep end of Beebe Lake, where Fall Creek enters that pond after having wended through picturesque Forest Home, just to the north. The braver swimmers would accept the challenge of jumping from the bridge into the stygian depths below. A bronze plaque on the bridge reads as follows: "The Beebe Lake Trail and this bridge were provided by a bequest which Henry Woodward Sackett of the class of 1875 made to Cornell University for the benefit of lovers of woodland beauty." Colonel Sackett's bequest was $200,000. Because of heavy silting in the shallow lake, the swimming pool was closed in the mid 1960's. In 1986 work began on removing the accumulated silt to make the pool once again available for swimmers.

70

Cornell's students of civil and other engineering disciplines have to learn about such matters as the technology and application of water turbines and the measurement of water flows. This lab, the first section of which was built in 1902, is where they get their training. Water normally flowing over the falls can be diverted into the canal seen at the right side of Beebe Lake, and then funnelled into the laboratory in whatever quantity is needed for the experiments to be performed. The picture's left side shows the north wall of Fall Creek gorge where a wooden framework supported a circular stairway. Triphammer Falls at the center of this picture can be a roaring cataract in the spring and is especially picturesque then.

Ithaca, N.Y.,
Hydraulic Laboratory, Triphammer falls.

Copyright 1906 by the Corner Book Stores.
Forest Home Walk, Cornell Campus, Ithaca, N. Y.

One of the most pleasant areas of the acres in the immediate vicinity of the Cornell campus proper is the region surrounding Beebe Lake. Forest Home Walk, which makes its way along the south side of the lake between Thurston Avenue and Forest Home, has provided many a restful hour for those who would traverse this woodsey trail to go to or from classes as students or, for those on the university payroll, to carry out a wide variety of professional responsibilities.

71

Prudence Risley was the mother-in-law of Russell Sage of New York, a family unrelated to the local Sages who had done so much for Cornell. Mrs. Russell Sage gave $300,000 for this memorial to her husband's mother, and its site north of the Fall Creek gorge was aided by the gift of $20,000 by a wealthy trustee, Emerson McMillin, in order to purchase the land. This was the university's second dormitory for women; it was designed by William H. Miller, and opened in 1912. Its main dining room was a particular source of interest to Andrew D.

PRUDENCE RISLEY HALL, CORNELL UNIVERSITY, ITHACA, N. Y.

White, as it was designed in the grand manner of an English collegiate hall. No sooner had this building been completed when architect Miller was called upon to design the new Ithaca High School, (see p. 9) to replace the one that burned in 1912. Note the architectural similarities between the two structures, most especially the towers and their battlements, suggesting that Mr. Miller transferred a bit of his design efforts from one building to the other.

BALCH HALL, CORNELL UNIVERSITY, ITHACA, N. Y

Balch Hall, a most beautiful dormitory for women, was the gift of Mr. and Mrs. Allen C. Balch, at a cost of $1,650,000; the first occupants moved in for the fall semester of 1929. The buildings in this complex, like many other on campus, are faced with native stone quarried near the university on Ellis Hollow Road, just north of Turkey Hill. Mr. Balch graduated from Cornell in 1889. Coeducation was a rather novel idea in the 1800's, and even well into this century the idea of having to share a campus with females was not universally well-accepted by male students.

It's obvious from this early scene that Cornell's Spring Day was much more than just a campus event, as thousands of townspeople line State Street to witness the parade. Late May is usually a pleasant time in these climes, and the risk of rain is small. Trucks have not yet replaced the teams of faithful horses which have before them a tough grind up the grades of State and Eddy Streets to gain access to Cornell.

This matched team of beautiful white horses (seen above in front of "The New Ithaca") approaches the top of their climb up East Hill for this Spring Day parade, as they and their float pass Cascadilla Hall and near the stone bridge over the gorge of the same name at the north end of College Avenue. Cleopatra's Barge could hardly have been lovelier than what these students have concocted for this display of revelry, near the end of the college year.

Spring Day, Ithaca, N. Y.

"Spring Day", held in late May, was a festive event on the Cornell Campus for many years. Here the activities are taking place on the quadrangle in front of White Hall. With stunts, games, intercollegiate and intramural sporting events, a parade, concerts by such luminaries as Sabela Wehe (the famed soprano with the golden voice) and a lot of general hoop-la, it was anxiously awaited by both University residents and all the small-fry of Ithaca.

Here's a typical side-show apparently perpetrated by a group of Cornell medical students, in front of Lincoln Hall during one of the 'Spring Days' early in the century, while at the right another group of 'performers' banters the assembled throng.

74

Here's how Cornellians appeared on Spring Day in 1910; most everyone has a smile, and it looks as though all are having a good time. Freshman 'beanies,' the required headgear for first-year students in those days and for many subsequent years, are very much in evidence. Heaven only knows what ridiculous performance was performed inside the tent; possibly a hula-dance show by a group of fraternity brothers dressed in female attire, or maybe a catch-the-greased-pig event. The whole day was one big frolic to permit students to 'let off steam' in a sort of Yankeeland "Mardi Gras".

College youths always seem to have to work off excess energy, and for years one way this was accomplished at Cornell was the annual Freshman-Sophomore rush, which took various forms as time progressed. The cameraman has done an admirable job of catching the spirit of the 1915-16 mud rush in this rare photo card where, in spite of the gooey mess, everyone seems to be having a good time. This type of antic has virtually disappeared, as college students today are generally a pretty serious bunch; it may well be that World War II was a turn-

ing point for activities of this nature . . . and it may also be that the current 'in' thing that has replaced it is to stage a demonstration or protest against some real or imagined social injustice.

Cornell's Armory and Gymnasium was designed by Charles Babcock, architect of Sage Chapel and other university facilities, and it was finished in 1883 at a cost of $31,300. It had three electric lighting fixtures which, according to Kermit Parsons, were the first on the campus. During the '30's the gymnasium was a popular roller skating rink. The structure was demolished in 1954 to make space for new engineering buildings. This card was posted on September 11, 1911, just after the beginning of the fall term, to Miss Winifred Hughes, 763 Ostrom Avenue, Syracuse, and included the following remark: "D, arrived here all ok. Am registered. Gee! but they sling the work at you here."

This scene is looking east on South Avenue, on the Armory green. The Cornellians we see here fulfilling their Army Reserve Officer Training Corps requirements (for long a standard part of the University's curriculum) would soon see action in World War 1. The names of those Cornellians who died in this awful conflict are set in stone in the cloisters of the War Memorial dormitory complex, with the exception of one Hans Wagner ('12) who served with the German forces.

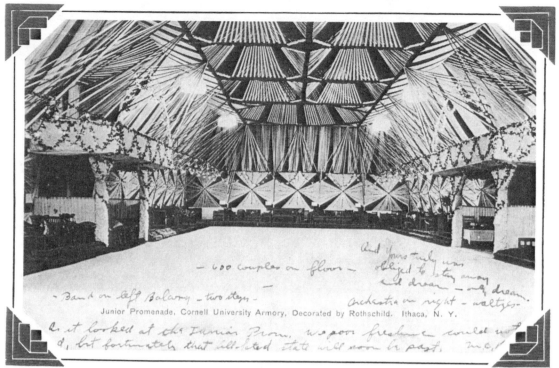

When Rothschild Brothers set out to decorate the old Armory for a Junior prom, they did it up right! The touching message of the young Freshman, who only dream of participating in this major campus event in the subsequent year, lends a nostalgic feeling to this scene of web-like bunting, crepe, spangles, and garlands assembled by the great downtown merchants. Notice that the writer refers to two groups of musicians—the band on the left balcony playing two-steps, and the orchestra on the right playing waltzes. For years the featured ensembles were Patsy Conway's band, and George Coleman's orchestra. Mr. Coleman was a member of the Cornell staff, and among other duties conducted the Cornell band; Conway was a famous bandmaster who held forth in Ithaca, and who was for years associated with the Ithaca Conservatory of Music, now Ithaca College.

According to Morris Bishop, "In 1899 Professor Fernow [of Forestry] was a member of the E. W. Harriman expedition to Alaska. In a deserted Tlingit village at Fox Cape the party found a superb totem pole. With much exertion and ingenuity they transported it to the ship and eventually to Cornell. It stood for about twenty years beside the old Armory, and after a period in hiding was in 1933 repaired, repainted, and set up, appropriately and impressively, before the lodge in Cornell's Arnot Forest." The Arnot Forest is 15 miles southwest of Ithaca, and is used for demonstration and laboratory work in forestry; it was given to Cornell by the heirs of Mathias Arnot of Elmira and has since been supplemented by other gifts of adjoining land.

Birds Eye View Percy Field, Cornell University, Ithaca, N. Y.

Today, Ithaca's High School occupies Percy Field, but starting in 1889 Cornell's athletic activities took place on these 9 acres of level ground, given to the university by William Sage. The name derives from Percy Hagerman ('90) whose father, J. J. Hagerman of Colorado Springs, gave $7,000 for the track and buildings. The location was far removed from and four hundred feet below the campus proper, and thus much less convenient than 'Alumni Field' which came into use around 1910. A most interesting aspect of this rare view is the yard of the street car lines, with various pieces of equipment standing in it, seen at the far edge of the ball field.

Athletes who participated in pole vaulting during the days of Jack Moakley's coaching, shown here at Percy Field, relied largely on sheer physical strength to make their way over the bar using a bamboo pole for assistance in gaining the necessary height. They broke their fall by dropping into sawdust, which offers little resiliency to a plunging body. Vaults of around 16 feet were eventually achieved in this manner, but when highly flexible fiberglas poles came into being, the sport changed dramatically. Today's vaulters rely much

more on their gymnastic ability to take advantage of the whip of the pole to top the bar. This technique, together with the advent of foam rubber, in place of sawdust, has helped push the record close to 20 feet.

John F. "Jack" Moakley joined the Cornell coaching staff in 1899 and stayed for fifty years, establishing a remarkable record of success in coaching track and field events. It is unlikely that athletes at Cornell, or any other college for that matter, will ever equal the string of victories achieved under his expert tutelage. During Moakley's tenure Cornell's achievements in field and track events were the envy of institutions all over America. Moakley House is dedicated in his memory; located at the golf course it serves as a field house, as well as a dormitory for visiting teams. The buildings in the background are the Percy Field facilities.

"JACK" MOAKLEY
Trainer of Cornell Track Team.

Cornell's athletic complex in this early scene includes the Schoellkopf Memorial Building (given by Willard Straight '01 in memory of Henry Schoellkopf '02), the stadium, and the Bacon baseball practice cage at the right. The family of Jacob Schoellkopf of Niagara Falls contributed to the development of the field and the stadium which was opened in 1915. The cage is named for George W. Bacon, class of '92, who was chairman of the Associate Alumni committee that raised the money for Alumni Field making it possible for athletic activities to be moved from distant Percy Field (on the Ithaca flatlands northwest of Ithaca Falls), to the campus proper. Schoellkopf Field resides on the corner of Hoy Field, named in honor of Cornell's first registrar, David Hoy, an ardent baseball fan. While heavily retouched by an artist, this card nevertheless captures the inherent beauty of the surrounding countryside with a view toward Turkey Hill and Mount Pleasant in the far distance.

...llkoph Memorial Building, Stadium and Baseball Cage, Cornell University, Ithaca,

CRESCENT AND SCHOELLKOFF MEMORIAL, ITHACA, N. Y.

On October 11, 1924, the new "Crescent" was formally opened with Cornell coach Gilmour Dobie's team pitted against Williams College. Gavin Hadden of New York was the engineer of the structure, which seats 21,500, and he provided an additional design for a comparable west side stand should it become necessary. One admirable feature of this shape, which features a row of private boxes around the top, is that a large proportion of spectators have a good view of the 50-yard line. In the printed program sold to spectators at the initial game were the usual ads for local businesses, and John P. Troy, the well-known photographer, stated in his that 'Exclusive Pictures and Postcards of this game will be on sale at the Co-op and other stores on Monday.' Note the then single stack of the university heating plant rising behind the Crescent; this facility was built between the time of this picture and the one at the bottom of page 79. Cornell's first President, Andrew D. White, was not a football fan, and in 1873 he would not authorize a game with the University of Michigan in Cleveland, stating "I refuse to let forty of our boys travel four hundred miles merely to agitate a bag of wind."

A 5208 Observatory, Cornell University, Ithaca, N. Y.

Barton Hall now occupies the site of the observatory seen in this picture with three domes to house instruments for heavenly scanning. It was replaced in the second decade of the 20th Century by the Fuertes Observatory located just north of Beebe Lake, where for many years what many consider the best Friday evening show in town (on clear nights only, of course) has traditionally been the "open to the public" chance to see the celestial bodies through the great 12 ½ inch refracting telescope. Your writer well recalls his astonishment as a little boy at seeing Saturn and its rings in vivid clarity through this telescope; the staff of the Department of Astronomy continues to delight in acquainting Cornellians and Ithacans with the wonders of the universe through this weekly activity. Today a more powerful telescope is located on Mt. Pleasant, east of the campus, but the refractor that was once housed here continues to do yeoman service in the teaching of astronomy.

This magnificent structure was seldom referred to in its earlier days as "The Armory", as this postcard would have us believe, the "Drill Hall" being the more common term until the time it was officially named for Colonel Frank Barton, ('91) in mechanical engineering. The building was built with $350,000 appropriated by the State Legislature in 1914, and was finished just in time to see plenty of service during World War I. Covering over two acres, for a time it was the largest drill hall on any campus in America. Barton was one of the first two reserve officers commissioned in the Army's Military Science program and he returned to the campus to command the ROTC unit from 1904 to 1908 and during the war years, just a decade later. The open automobile styles, together with what appears to be a "racer-bodied" Model T Ford or something similar at the extreme right, suggest that the picture was taken not long after the building came into use.

ARMORY, CORNELL UNIVERSITY, ITHACA, N. Y.

An event happily long forgotten, but a nice interior view of "The New Armory" — Barton Hall. This vast expanse has since 1915 provided Cornellians with a place for many activities in addition to military drills. Basketball games, proms, mass registration for classes; anything that required lots of floor space. For many years an enormous British military tank from World War 1 occupied the far corner, but unfortunately from the point of view of anyone interested in war collectibles, it disappeared some years ago. Apparently university officials simply got tired of looking at and having to work around what was essentially a useless pile of iron, and disposed of it when nobody was looking. How they got it out of the building and hauled it away is a matter of conjecture except to those few who were in on the act! The building was four years old when this card was postmarked in 1919.

THE HARDLY FAIR" NEW ARMORY, MARCH. 8, 19-MOTTO-"THE PUBLIC BE REAMED

81

For many years the Annual Dress parade in the late spring of the year was a standard feature of the ROTC program at Cornell, with the university's President in black tails and top hat and the Commanding General of the First Army reviewing the cadets from their vantage point in front of Goldwin Smith Hall. At least this was the format when your writer was a Cadet Captain in charge of a company of Freshman and Sophomores, and the dress uniform was a bit more modern than in this pre-1907 card — witness the magnificent headgear

worn by that early band. An unforgettable incident on that later occasion in 1948 took place when the always irreverent students of the School of Architecture burst forth from the doors of White Hall in company formation, dressed in ragtag clothes, and marched onto the quad behind their standard-bearer holding high a guidon consisting of a five-foot wide floor mop! The campus police quickly broke up their merry prank so they caused a minimum of disruption to the military formalities. If the General and the President were disturbed by this minor affront to the dignity of the larger event, they didn't let on. Architecture students worked hard over the years to maintain their image of fun-loving buffoonery, at times to the administration's dismay.

These graduating seniors seem eager to get on with their academic procession, accept their diplomas, and get out into the real world after long years of study at a university that has never been known as an easy place to "pick up a degree". It was seventy years before this book was written that these faces passed the ten-year-old Goldwin Smith Hall, and surviving members of that class would by now be in their late 80's or early 90's. Regrettably, this is the class that immediately faced entry into World War I, and many that served in that conflict would also participate in World War II.

Stone, Roberts, and East Roberts Halls were dedicated in 1907, the first major buildings on the new agricultural campus; Comstock Hall is at the far left in this view. Stone was the home of the department of Rural Education; Roberts, named for Dean Isaac Roberts, was the administration building for agriculture, and East Roberts was the new dairy building, supplanting the earlier one which became part of Goldwin Smith Hall. In the early pre-radar days of World War II, the government established a network of air-raid spotting posts, manned by civilian volunteers who listened for airplanes and telephoned their reports to a "filter center" somewhere in the eastern U.S.A. Presumably this system was patterned after the British experience in fending off raids by Hitler's aerial armadas; history does not record any actual prevention having occured here in the States. A small cabin was erected for this purpose on top of Roberts Hall, and as a teenager your writer stood a number of two-person night watches with Professsor Morris Bishop, Cornell's historian, and later Sarah Gibson Blanding, the dean of Home Economics who went on to become President of Vassar, the college for women in Poughkeepsie, New York. As this book is written, a battle rages between campus developers and local preservationists as to the fate of these buildings.

The architect for Cornell's first building devoted to veterinary science was Charles Osborne. This building, James Law Hall, was opened in 1894. Law was Cornell's first Professor of Veterinary Medicine. This yellow brick structure and the others which were associated with it were demolished 65 years later to make room for the School of Industrial and Labor Relations; veterinary school activities were moved east to a new and elaborate facility at the end of Tower Road.

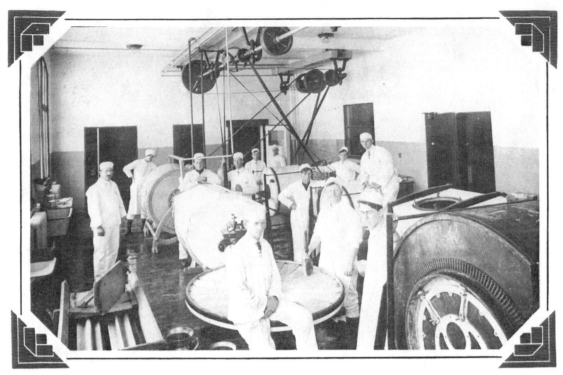

Stocking Hall, labelled "The Dairy Building", seen on the left, was opened in 1923. As a by-product of training students in the fields of dairy science and dairy industry, the manufacture and sale of ice cream made addicts of generations of Ithacans and Cornellians for the first-class product of the facility located in this building. In the scene above, students in the pre-OSHA days of open line shafts and flat leather belting take a moment from their practical studies of the technology of the dairy business to pose in their white uniforms in Stocking Hall's sanitary environment. Henry H. Wing ('81) established the department of animal husbandry, and the building on the right which bears his name—although not stated on this view—came into being in 1913. The earlier buildings on the agricultural campus, while not distinguished from an architectural standpoint, have traditionally been named for well-known and outstanding members of the faculty. William B. Stocking ('98)was one of many who have served the university well, and was so honored. Herbert Hoover once said that "the greatest honor that an American can have is for a school to be named named for him." Implied in this statement is that a school building offers comparable recognition.

Dairy and Animal Husbandry Buildings, Cornell University.   Ithaca, N. Y.

Home Economics Building, Cornell University, Ithaca, N. Y.

Comstock Hall, built to house the Department of Home Economics, came into being about the same time as Fernow, Rice, Wing, and Caldwell Halls, which explains, since they were all the products of the State Architect's office around 1912, why they are so similar. Anna Botsford Comstock ('86) and her husband John Henry Comstock ('74) were two of the most influential people ever to set foot on the Cornell campus. She was the first woman on the faculty to hold professorial rank (albeit temporarily), and he started, while still an undergraduate, the first Department of Entomology in any American university . . . in addition to which John Comstock was chimesmaster. In 1893 the couple founded the Comstock Publishing Company, and one of its great successes was Mrs. Comstock's book *Handbook of Nature Study* which went many printings. Her husband was co-author of *Introduction to Entomology* with Simon Gage, which was the first book published by the firm. It was a highly successful venture, and they willed it to Cornell which took it over in 1931. It became an important foundation of The Cornell University Press, whose headquarters is in the Comstock home at 124 Roberts Place, on the edge of Fall Creek gorge.

MARTHA VAN RENSSELAER HALL, CORNELL UNIVERSITY, ITHACA, N. Y.

Miss Van Rensellaer had been the School Commissioner of Cattaraugus County, a job she left to initiate at Cornell a reading course for farmer's wives. After acquiring a B.S. degree in 1909, she became in 1911 one of the first two women professors at the university, and the co-director, with Miss Flora Rose, of the Department of Home Economics. In 1913 Comstock Hall was opened to house the ever-growing department, yet within 20 years a larger facility was badly needed. Two weeks after the death of Martha Van Rensellaer, the cornerstone of the building bearing her name was laid, and it opened for educational activity in the fall of 1933. When Martha Van Rensselaer Hall was built it was without doubt the finest building of its type in the nation, with extraordinary equipment and facilities to back up the teaching efforts of its staff. The term "Home Economics" has been replaced in recent years by "Human Ecology."

Bailey Hall, named for Liberty Hyde Bailey—the professor and administrator who had so much influence in the development of the College of Agriculture—opened in 1913. Since then it has served all the usual purposes of an auditorium, but is probably best-remembered by Cornellians and Ithacans for housing musical events featuring prominent orchestras, bands, and artists from all over the world. The pipe organ was given by Andrew Carnegie as a tribute to Cornell's first President, Andrew D. White. The locals in the 1930's and 40's were surprised to learn that most United States citizens were unaware that President Franklin D. Roosevelt was a victim of infantile paralysis, unable to walk. When he was New York's Governor, he gave a talk each year in Bailey Hall during "Farm and Home Week" and a ramp, plainly evident, was constructed to permit him to maneuver up to the entrance. The small building behind the Lua A. Minns Memorial Garden was built as a model schoolhouse by the Rural Education Department; when New York State schools were consolidated it became redundant, and in the 1930's it served as the campus studio of WESG, the Elmira Star-Gazette radio station whose transmitter was near Forest Home. Frank E. Gannett operated the Elmira paper; it formed the basis of today's giant newspaper chain bearing his name.

NEW YORK HOSPITAL—CORNELL MEDICAL COLLEGE ASSOCIATION BUILDINGS. NEW YORK CITY 15

Cornell's involvement in training medical doctors goes back to the late 1800's, and its great benefactor over the years was Colonel Oliver Payne whose father was one of the founders of the Standard Oil Company. He paid for a facility in New York City where students studied and learned in cooperation with Bellevue Medical Center. At this time students were able to get their first two years of schooling on the Ithaca campus, a policy discontinued in 1938. In the 'twenties Payne Whitney, who was an heir to his uncle Oliver's money, gave several million dollars toward the construction of the New York Hospital- Cornell Medical College which opened in 1932. The affiliation with the New York Hospital that made this a practical reality had taken place in 1927. The Cornell Medical School took bold strides in those days as a leader in training nurses within the framework of a university, as compared with the more traditional schooling for this worthy profession.

This crude building is Cornell's first hydroelectric power plant, in Fall Creek. Its successor was built in 1904, and today, after a $1.3 million rebuilding project in 1979-80, the falling waters generate about 5% of the university's electricity needs. The power is sold to the New York State Electric and Gas Corporation as a credit against Cornell's 8-million-dollar per year electric bill, and a little arithmetic will show that the renovation was indeed an excellent investment. The plant's new cross-flow turbines are German-made Ossburger machines

Copyright 1905 by the Rotograph Co.
H 5187 Fall Creek, Ithaca, N. Y.

which turn at 300 rpm, geared to drive American-built Reliance generators at 1250 rpm which are capable of putting out 1 ½ megawatts, should enough water flow. This is a high-tech operation, with closed circuit TV monitoring and a visit by a technician to check things out about once a week. The location is just north of Sibley Hall, almost underneath today's famous suspension bridge. Such bridges have long been part of the Cornell scene; the one seen here was the first walkway across Fall Creek gorge built especially to accomodate faculty and students.

There's nothing like falling water to produce cheap electricity. but water isn't always available so the builders of the Fall Creek power plant, which was constructed in 1892-93 right below Stewart Avenue, also provided steam boilers to spin the generators. A 70-foot head of water made it possible to generate 800 horsepower as long as water flowed in adequate volume. This plant, which is not to be confused with Cornell's water-power plant a few hundred yards up the gorge (see the picture above), supplied electrical energy to the Ithaca

Fall Creek Gorge, Ithaca, N. Y.

Handcolored.

Street Railway Company as well as to other users of power. In 1901 a December flood damaged this plant, and thereafter the railway for many years got its power from a steam plant associated with the Remington Salt Works located on the east shore just north of the head of Cayuga Lake. In 1905 the entire Fall Creek plant was destroyed by fire.

Suspension Bridge from Cornell Campus to Cornell He. over Ithaca Gorge. Ithaca, N. Y.

In 1900 the Cornell Heights Land Company built this suspension bridge, a pedestrian walkway, for the obvious purpose of enhancing the value of the lots they were selling on the north side of Fall Creek gorge. With a large ratio of span to width, and of light construction as befits a load of only people and an occasional bicycle, it was easy for daredevils to get it swaying a good bit to thrill the acrophobic and it was, in fact, popularly known as Fall Creek's "swinging bridge." The suspension members were eyebars, probably of wrought iron. In recent years a replacement went into service; it hangs from steel cables. The penstock at the left appears to have been the one that provided a 70-foot head of water for the power house which supplied electrical energy for the trolley company, and for other uses, almost underneath the Stewart Avenue bridge. Notice the swimmers enjoying a dip on this pleasant summer day, and the spectators on the bridge enjoying the scenery.

Upper Bridge over Fall Creek, Ithaca, N. Y.

There was no way for vehicles to cross Fall Creek gorge until Triphammer Bridge, of steel arch construction, was built in 1897 to connect Thurston Avenue on the north and East Avenue on the south. Because the road deck is on the top of the arch, the view from the road or walkways is completely clear, offering a fine vantage point from which to witness Beebe Lake, its dam, the hydraulic lab of Cornell's civil engineering department on the east, and the splendor of the gorge itself on the west. The bridge was built by a group of land developers, headed by Edward G. Wyckoff ('89). The trolley line crossed it making its way past the spot where the Prudence Risley dorm would rise a dozen years later, down the length of Thurston Avenue to "The Knoll" and thence to the Stewart Avenue bridge to return across the gorge and back to the city proper.

Bridge over Fall Creek, Ithaca, N. Y.

The Stewart Avenue Bridge over Fall Creek is a wonderful vantage point for a view overlooking the end of Cayuga Lake and the flatlands of ethaca. A famous episode in one of the early movies filmed in Ithaca involved a disused trolley car (No. 305, which had started its life in 1892 as a 3rd Avenue cable car in New York City) crashing through the guard rail of the bridge and into the gorge below. As noted elsewhere, the Wharton Studios, producers of various movies and serials which thrilled nickelodeon audiences all over America was based in Renwick Park for about five years. J. P. Troy, who copyrighted this photo in 1906, was a prominent local photographer. Note on the upper card the horse and wagon on the bridge just ahead of the trolley car which, incidentally, has had its energy-supplying overhead wires removed by the retoucher. The message on this card, written in 1913 to Miss Jennie Fraser of 181 W. 102nd St., New York City, is as follows: "Dear Jennie. How'd you like to fall from this bridge. s/May. Dandy up here." Ah well; such is the glorious prose of which post card correspondence is made. The lower card clearly shows the dam, gone for many years, and what appears to be the remains of the power house seen in the lower picture on page 87.

HAPPY NEW YEAR TOBOGGAN SLIDE, CORNELL UNIVERSITY CAMPUS ITHACA, N.Y.

The toboggan slide on Beebe Lake's south shore provided countless hours of pleasure for Cornellians and Ithacans alike during its many years of existence, starting early in this Century. The moustachioed chap at the front of the lead toboggan appears to be working hard to maintain a professorial demeanor as he and his companions whisk out onto the frozen lake. The slide was a constant source of worry to university officials due to possible injuries to its users, and in fact there were quite a number of bruises and fractured vertebrae reported over the years to the health services. The slide was removed in the 1939-40 season. This scene appears on many postcards in various formats, of which this greeting card is a most interesting version. Specialized cards such as those for Christmas and Easter provide themes for collectors who like to build something unique within their holdings.

VINTER SCENE, TRIPHAMMER FALLS, ITHACA, N.Y.

There is no denying that old man winter can create some lovely scenes around a place as pretty as the Cornell Campus, and Triphammer Falls with its surrounding dam and hydraulic laboratories with their characteristically glacial appearance during January and February is a case in point. Soon, of course, the spring thaws will take over to make the whole affair a muddy and murky scene.

TAUGHANNOCK FALL

In the mid-'twenties New York State, beginning with 54 acres, created a park surrounding Taughannock Falls, (at 215 feet one of America's highest east of the Rockies). Other donations and purchases have since brought the total to 738 acres. The stone masonry lookout point in this scene, constructed during the 1930's, provides a wonderful vantage point from which to view the slim cataract. During severe winters a large cone of ice often develops at the base of the falls, sometimes reaching as much as a third of its height, and always provoking a lot of extra sightseeing by the locals wanting to see the latest of nature's wonders. In the 1800's the power of the falling waters was used for a variety of purposes, among them a substantial mill just west of the falls which was washed away in the 1935 flood (as was a brand new park pavilion next to the creek on the flatlands below, close to Cayuga Lake). At one time there were two hotels—one located near this look-out, and the other on the south side of the gorge close to the falls. This latter one was used, for a time, as a tuberculosis hospital.

Ithaca, N.Y. Taughannock Gorge.

The full beauty of the deep gorge between Taughannock Falls and Cayuga Lake is especially apparent to those who take the time to walk its length, as the area is only partially visible from the highway or the observation point above and opposite to the falls itself. As in all such cleavages of the earth's surface, most of us find difficulty in relating to the eons required for a relatively small meandering stream to cut through hundreds of feet of rock on its way to lower levels.

Buttermilk Falls, with a fine swimming pool at its base, is the closest state park to Ithaca, and gets plenty of use by those seeking a pleasant spot on a summer's day for a picnic, or perhaps for some camping. Hiking the gorge trails is fine recreation during good weather; cross-country skiing in the winter is for those who enjoy being out when fahrenheits are in short supply. The park's origin dates to 1924 when Mr. and Mrs. Robert Treman donated 154 acres for creation of a park; additional acquisitions bring the total to 751 acres. Treman Lake is in the upper part of the gorge and near it there was once an impoundment from which the Ithaca Water Works Company (a privately-owned organization) supplied water to the City of Ithaca from 1875 to 1912.

Buttermilk Falls, Enfield Glen, and Taughannock Falls get all the publicity because they have been taken over as state parks. There are also many lesser-known glens, waterfalls and ravines around Ithaca which are marvels of natural beauty. Lick Brook near Buttermilk Falls is a good example. Cascadilla and Fall Creek Gorges which form the east and west boundaries of the Cornell Campus are two others; Six-Mile Creek from which Ithaca derives its water supply is another; there is also Coy Glen across the valley from Buttermilk Falls. Cornell geology students have ample reason to spend time on field trips in the area as their learned professors explain how our terrain has developed over the centuries, and what effects the great glacier of some 20,000 years ago had in shaping this attractive region.

92

IMMING POOL, BUTTERMILK FALLS, NEAR ITHACA, N.Y.

Close proximity to Ithaca makes the swimming pool at Buttermilk Falls a popular one. When the park was developed there was a great demand for recreational facilities such as this one in our public parks.

Washington Park, adjacent to West Buffalo Street, was created by Simeon DeWitt and his son Richard Varick DeWitt in 1832 as a residential section adjacent to the commercial part of the city and to schools. The grounds were taken over by the community trustees during the administration of Nathan T. Williams in 1847, and the park has been protected by municipal law ever since. Today we are indebted to this group of public officials who were sufficiently farsighted to reserve from development some space for children to play, for se-

Washington Park, Ithaca, N.Y.

niors to relax, and for the local bands in the earlier part of this century to have a place for marching practice. The gazebo is long gone. Its purpose is not clear as it's too small for a bandstand; perhaps it was intended to accomodate a summertime foursome for whist or euchre, two popular card games of an earlier era.

Falls, Ithaca, N.Y.

"Enfield" appears on all the post cards in this book related to what is now Robert H. Treman State Park, because they were all published prior to 1938 when, following Mr. Treman's death, the park was re-named in his honor. He and his wife had given 387 acres of the site to the state for park development in 1920, and when the Finger Lakes State Park Commission was formed in 1924, Treman was put in charge. Today the park encompasses 1025 acres of glen and stream, numerous waterfalls of which Enfield Falls (with its swimming hole at the base) is the most prominent, two camping areas 3 miles apart, an old mill, picnic areas, and the most pleasant and peaceful surroundings anyone could want.

This view of a rickety wooden trail clinging to the cliff wall of Enfield Gorge is hardly designed to instill confidence in the would-be visitor! During the great depression of the 1930's the Federal Government established the Civilian Conservation Corps, primarily to put young unemployed men to work at constructive tasks all over the country. Some 1450 CCC Camps were established across the country; they were run by military officers, and there was one near here. However, instead of performing military drills the men worked at such jobs as reforestation, park development, and the construction of miles of safe walkways and stone bridges through glens and gorges to replace the sort of thing we see here. Your writer was privileged to know a number of men during his World War II service who had served in CCC Camps, and he never knew any of them to think that it had been anything other than a fine and worthwhile experience. Note that this pre-1907 card states "Along the Lehigh", which means that it was intended to promote passenger service on the Lehigh Valley Railroad which operated between New York City and Buffalo.

Enfield Gorge, Ithaca, N.Y., Along the Lehigh

America developed along its watercourses, when illumination was still from whale oil lamps, and the horse was the prime mover for land transportation. The availability of energy from falling waters was most important, and this fine old mill in the upper section of Robert H. Treman State Park is wonderfully preserved to show ours and succeeding generations how our forefathers ground corn and wheat into flour to feed a growing nation. The mill was built in 1839, and there were several industrial buildings surrounding it,

OLD MILL, ENFIELD FALLS STATE PARK, N.Y.

along with a hotel, in the 1870's. In a brochure published by the Finger Lakes State Park Commission we are told that the mill has main floor beams fourteen inches square and thirty-six feet long, each hewn from a single log. Oak pegs were used to pin the structure together, a method of construction that has stood the test of time.

PARKING AREA, OLD MILL, ENFIELD FALLS   ITHACA, N. Y.

Indicative of the long-time popularity of Enfield Falls State Park and especially the old mill in the upper section of that facility is this large group of cars in the parking area. Closed body automobiles were becoming popular in the early 1920's, and Detroit's new "streamlined" styling was begun in the early 1930's. This scene must therefore date from the mid or late 1920's, and car buffs may enjoy the challenge of identifying the makes and models seen here.

95

Family camping endures as a favorite American recreation. When this scene was photographed at Enfield Falls back in the 'twenties, it was a time when the average working man could begin to think about affording an automobile, and when he finally owned one, he had to put it to use taking the family somewhere. It was a time when we began the habit of "hitting the road" to get out of the cities and drove across the land to see new vistas on vacations, an activity previously reserved for the well-to-do. For those who could not afford hotel accomodations, camping put travel within reach.

The picturesque setting of the impounding facility for the water to operate the old mill at Robert H. Treman State Park makes for a most attractive postcard. One wonders how many of these were sent to Aunt Minnie or cousin Flora three generations ago when the card was first published, with such endearing messages as "wish you were here", or "having a wonderful time".

More early postcards are seen featuring Enfield Falls State Park than any other of the state parks in the Ithaca region. This is perhaps due to the fact that its scenic beauties are spread out over a wide area, thus affording a greater number of photo opportunities, than do Buttermilk Falls, Taughannock Falls, and others which focus on a single major attraction. The Narrows, a section of the glen between the upper and lower sections of the park, can be seen only by those who take the time to traverse the lovely gorge trail which exposes the beauties of nature for all who care to see.

The substantial stone steps leading up the side of the gorge adjacent to Lucifer Falls, a magnificent waterfall in Enfield Gorge in Robert H. Treman State Park, were built during the CCC era of the 1930's. They offer a much more secure and less risky route to those who would make the hike through the gorge than did the flimsy board walkway of an earlier time, as seen on the "Enfield Gorge along the Lehigh" postcard on page 94.

S AT LUCIFER FALLS. ENFIELD GLEN STATE PARK, N.Y.

Thousands of Boy Scouts have enjoyed Camp Barton, 13 miles north of Ithaca. Those who attended between 1927 and 1968 (when this structure was razed) have fond memories of the headquarters building that is seen here when it was the Frontenac Hotel. The hotel was built around 1870; in 1887 new owners renamed it for the famed steamboat. It is said to have been a popular place for Cornell students, but its patronage waned as the lake boats disappeared and it was sold in 1915 for $1600. In 1922 Camp Barton was established at Taughannock Point, a mile south, but in 1927 New York took over that land for a state park. The Boy Scout Council then bought the hotel and 89 acres with 3000 feet of frontage in 1927 for $14,600, the amount being covered in a 1929 fund drive which paid for Camp Barton and also provided some funding for nearby Camp Comstock, the Girl Scout camp. Colonel Frank A. Barton, for whom the camp is named, was an early leader in the area's scout movement. Barton Hall on the Cornell campus was also named for him.

Little known to the general public is this splendid 120-foot waterfall in Trumansburg Creek's gorge that marks the northern border of Camp Barton. Highway 89 passes almost directly over the top of the falls, and those who would stop for a moment and get out of their car for a look-see are treated to a fine view from the bridge, looking downwards and east toward the lake. In the spring of the year when waters are running strong it can be a truly wondrous sight.

Cayuga Lake, N.Y., Falls of Frontenac Beach.

ONE OF THE SEVEN VILLAGES AT CAMP BARTON

Camp Barton's camping areas are called "villages". Each contains several tent platforms, and they're named for Indian tribes such as Cayuga, Seneca, etc. Every Boy Scout who comes to summer camp for the first time quickly learns that it's not all fun and games, and that there is work to be done such as policing the area to keep the grounds tidy and neat, all part of citizenship training. Chances are these two boys are in the "Tenderfoot" classification, and on their way to earning merit badges to carry them up the ranks to second class, first class, and maybe eventually they'll even become Eagle Scouts. It's a great learning experience for the young, one your writer can heartily recommend from having done it for several summers in his youth.

Anna Botsford Comstock ('85), long remembered for her work as a naturalist, was Cornell's first woman to hold professorial rank. Though not a Girl Scout herself (she came along before the scout movement became popular), she was an enthusiastic supporter of the Girl Scouts and served on their national advisory committee for nature study. When the camp at Crowbar Point, 9 miles north of Ithaca on Cayuga Lake's west shore was established in 1927, (thanks to a gift of land by Professor and Mrs. Ernest T. Paine who had purchased

it from a grandaughter of Ezra Cornell) it was a natural to name the camp after Comstock — who had been named as "One of the 12 greatest women in America" by the League of Women Voters in 1923. The Ithaca Zonta Club was instrumental in raising money to help equip the camp, and in 1929 the Boy and Girl Scouts cooperated in a campaign to raise $53,000 which helped ease the remaining burden of debt. Generations of girls since that time have sung "Just a Camp at Crowbar" to the tune of "Just a Song at Twilight": "Just a camp at Crowbar/ Just a Girl Scout Camp/ Anna Botsford Comstock/ 'mid the dew and damp/. But the camp we're loving/ to which we'll all be true/ Camp Anna Botsford Comstock/ Hear us sing to you — oh hear us sing to you."

Let's sail 'round the moon and then stop at

ITHACA, N. Y.

for refreshments.

"Aeroplanes" were favorite subjects for artists of "gag" cards back around 1914 when this card was postmarked. The chap who designed this one was a bit off in his judgment of what it would eventually take to fly around the moon, but aircraft of his day were still glorified box-kites and he's close to the mark as to their general appearance. In 1914 Ithaca was about to become a center for aircraft manufacturing, so the scene is appropriate . . . but frequently marginal weather conditions worked against the prospect of the community ever developing a major factor aeronautical industry. Ithaca was served for many years by the field at the head of Cayuga Lake, where a substantial hangar—now the "Hangar Theatre"—was built in the early 1930's. During World War II it was obvious that this small facility would not meet the growing aviation needs of the area, so Cornell University invested in the property that eventually would became today's Tompkins County Airport. And Sunday fliers like those on this card are always welcome to drop in for a cup of coffee or other refreshments.

One might be tempted to suggest this scene is on the shores of Cayuga Lake, but obviously it's one of those "gag" cards that were applied universally to whatever community the postcard publisher was pitching his sales at the time. Using a big log for a trysting place seems a bit precarious, but this was before the days of closed automobiles, and this couple had to do the best they could. People always manage to find a way!

I'M MAKING AN IMPRESSION

IN ITHACA, N. Y.

Bibliography: some basic works

Abt, Henry E. ITHACA. R. W. Kellogg, 1926.

Lee, Hardy Campbell. A HISTORY OF THE RAILROADS IN TOMPKINS COUNTY. DeWitt Historical Society of Tompkins County, 1947.

Bishop, Morris. A HISTORY OF CORNELL. Cornell University Press, 1962.

Robinson, Bob. CAYUGA LAKE BOATING. 1965.

Young, Charles V. P. CORNELL IN PICTURES — the first century. Quill and Dagger Alumni Association, 1965.

Parsons, Kermit Carlyle. THE CORNELL CAMPUS. Cornell University Press, 1968.

Heidt, William Jr. and Kammen, Carol. SIMEON DeWITT — FOUNDER OF ITHACA. DeWitt Historical Society, 1968.

Kerr, Richard D. THE ITHACA STREET RAILWAY. Harold E. Cox, 1972.

Archer, Robert F. A HISTORY OF THE LEHIGH VALLEY RAILROAD. Howell-North Books, 1977.

Tabers, (The) Thomas (father and son). THE DELAWARE, LACKAWANNA, AND WESTERN RAILROAD (in three volumes). Thomas Taber III, 1977, 1980. 1981.

White, John H., Jr. THE AMERICAN RAILWAY PASSENGER CAR. Johns Hopkins University Press, 1978.

Snodderly, Daniel R. ITHACA AND ITS PAST. DeWitt Historical Society of Tompkins County, 1982.

Connell, John. MR. CORNELL'S RAILROAD AND HOW IT GREW. Grapevine Press, 1982.

Harcourt, John B. THE ITHACA COLLEGE STORY. Ithaca College, 1983.

Kammen, Carol. THE PEOPLING OF TOMPKINS COUNTY: A SOCIAL HISTORY. Heart of the Lakes Publishing, 1985.

Stinson, Donald J. THE BURNING OF THE FRONTENAC. Heart of the Lakes Publishing, 1985.